Learning SaltStack

Second Edition

Build, manage, and secure your infrastructure by
utilizing the power of SaltStack

Colton Myers

BIRMINGHAM - MUMBAI

Learning SaltStack

Second Edition

First published: January 2015

Second edition: June 2016

Production reference: 1270616

Published by Packt Publishing Ltd.
Livery Place
35 Livery Street
Birmingham B3 2PB, UK.

ISBN 978-1-78588-190-9

www.packtpub.com

Credits

Author
Colton Myers

Reviewer
Joseph Hall

Commissioning Editor
Pratik Shah

Acquisition Editor
Divya Poojari

Content Development Editor
Rashmi Suvarna

Technical Editors
Manali Gonsalves
Novina Kewalramani
Pramod Kumavat

Copy Editor
Dipti Mankame

Project Coordinator
Judie Jose

Proofreader
Safis Editing

Indexer
Hemangini Bari

Graphics
Kirk D'Penha

Production Coordinator
Shantanu N. Zagade

Cover Work
Shantanu N. Zagade

About the Author

Colton Myers is a software engineer living in Salt Lake City, Utah. Since graduating with a BS in Computer Science from the University of Utah, he has worked professionally, writing software in Python. He loves working on open source software and has made multiple appearances as a speaker at the US PyCon conference.

Colton is a SaltStack Certified Trainer and has worked on the Salt open source software for years. He was previously a core engineer at SaltStack. At the time this book was published, he was a Python developer and systems engineer at Adobe.

Find him on Twitter and Github at `@basepi`.

I would like to thank my friends and family for the support they've given me as I've written this book. I'd also like to thank Tom Hatch for creating such kick-ass software, and growing a fantastic company and community. Finally, I'd like to thank the SaltStack community; without them, SaltStack would be nothing.

About the Reviewer

Joseph Hall is a Senior Cloud Engineer at SaltStack. His contributions inside Salt include a number of execution modules, cloud modules, and the creation of both SDB and SPM. He is also the author of *Mastering SaltStack* and *Extending SaltStack*, both by Packt Publishing.

www.PacktPub.com

eBooks, discount offers, and more

Did you know that Packt offers eBook versions of every book published, with PDF and ePub files available? You can upgrade to the eBook version at www.PacktPub.com and as a print book customer, you are entitled to a discount on the eBook copy. Get in touch with us at customercare@packtpub.com for more details.

At www.PacktPub.com, you can also read a collection of free technical articles, sign up for a range of free newsletters and receive exclusive discounts and offers on Packt books and eBooks.

https://www2.packtpub.com/books/subscription/packtlib

Do you need instant solutions to your IT questions? PacktLib is Packt's online digital book library. Here, you can search, access, and read Packt's entire library of books.

Why subscribe?

- Fully searchable across every book published by Packt
- Copy and paste, print, and bookmark content
- On demand and accessible via a web browser

Table of Contents

Preface

SaltStack (or Salt, for short) is an open source project that was started by Thomas Hatch in 2011. It was originally intended to be a lightning-fast remote execution system. Later, the various pieces that make up the Salt that we know today were added on top of this flexible layer. Salt is now one of the most popular open source projects in the world and one of the most popular infrastructure management platforms.

The project is managed by SaltStack, Inc., a company dedicated to preserving the open source nature of the software. SaltStack, Inc. provides service, long-term support, and custom code in their enterprise product, and supports the open source Salt project with a team of dedicated engineers.

Why do you care? What can Salt do for you?

Salt is the easiest, most powerful way to manage your servers. Whether you have a few, hundreds, or even tens of thousands of servers, you can use Salt to manage them from a single central point. You can use it to flexibly target any subset of your servers to run commands or accomplish tasks. You can use the state system to define the state of your infrastructure in a data-driven way and then enforce that state in seconds, with a single command. You can even create a reactive, self-healing infrastructure using the event system. Salt is written in Python and designed to be easy to extend for your own specific use-cases or purposes.

We're going to learn how to do all this and more in these pages. By the end of this book, you will have the knowledge you need to begin making the management of your infrastructure easier with Salt.

Let's get to it!

What this book covers

Chapter 1, Diving In – Our First Salt Commands, will discuss how to install Salt and execute basic commands.

Chapter 2, Controlling Your Minions with Remote Execution, will show how to use Salt to accomplish tasks on your minions through remote execution.

Chapter 3, Execution Modules – Write Your Own Solution, will discuss how to write your own custom remote execution modules to extend Salt for your own purposes.

Chapter 4, Defining the State of Your Infrastructure, will discuss how to use Salt States to define and enforce the state of your infrastructure.

Chapter 5, Expanding Our States with Jinja2 and Pillar, will discuss how to make your states more flexible and powerful by using Jinja2 and Pillar data.

Chapter 6, The Highstate and Environments, will show how to structure your states into environments and enforce the state of your entire infrastructure using a single command.

Chapter 7, Using Salt Cloud to Manage Virtual Minions, will show how to manage your cloud virtual machines using salt-cloud to create and manage VMs.

Chapter 8, The Reactor and the Event System, will show how to make your infrastructure automatically react to changes by using the reactor and event system built into Salt.

Chapter 9, Security Best Practices in Salt, will show how to secure your SaltStack infrastructure from attackers.

Chapter 10, How Can I Get Involved?, will show how to go beyond this book and learn more about Salt, as well as how to get involved in the SaltStack community.

What you need for this book

You will need access to a Linux machine to run the examples in this book. The preferred operating system is Ubuntu 14.04, but any major distribution of Linux is acceptable. If you use an operating system other than Ubuntu 14.04, your output may differ from the example output in the book.

Who this book is for

The biggest target audience for this book is system administrators. However, anyone who works with servers, whether application/web developers, system administrators, or hobbyists, will be able to use to this book to learn how to manage their servers/infrastructure easily and consistently.

No prior Salt knowledge is assumed. However, even Salt veterans will find new knowledge and best practices to apply in their own infrastructures. This book is for anyone who wants to better manage their infrastructure with Salt.

Conventions

In this book, you will find a number of text styles that distinguish between different kinds of information. Here are some examples of these styles and an explanation of their meaning.

Code words in text, database table names, folder names, filenames, file extensions, pathnames, dummy URLs, user input, and Twitter handles are shown as follows: "Now, you must open the file /etc/apt/sources.list and add the following line."

A block of code is set as follows:

```
test_state
  file.managed:
    - name: /tmp/test.txt
    - source: salt://test.txt
    - user: root
    - group: root
    - mode: 644
```

When we wish to draw your attention to a particular part of a code block, the relevant lines or items are set in bold:

```
test_state
  file.managed:
    - name: /tmp/test.txt
    - source: salt://test.txt
    - user: root
    - group: root
    - mode: 644
```

Any command-line input or output is written as follows:

```
# cp /usr/src/asterisk-addons/configs/cdr_mysql.conf.sample
    /etc/asterisk/cdr_mysql.conf
```

New terms and **important words** are shown in bold. Words that you see on the screen, for example, in menus or dialog boxes, appear in the text like this: "Continue the installation process by clicking **Next** and agreeing to the license agreement."

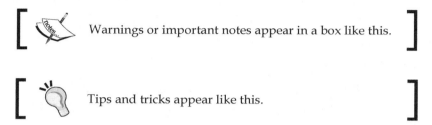

Warnings or important notes appear in a box like this.

Tips and tricks appear like this.

Reader feedback

Feedback from our readers is always welcome. Let us know what you think about this book—what you liked or disliked. Reader feedback is important for us as it helps us develop titles that you will really get the most out of.

To send us general feedback, simply e-mail feedback@packtpub.com, and mention the book's title in the subject of your message.

If there is a topic that you have expertise in and you are interested in either writing or contributing to a book, see our author guide at www.packtpub.com/authors.

Customer support

Now that you are the proud owner of a Packt book, we have a number of things to help you to get the most from your purchase.

Downloading the example code

You can download the example code files for this book from your account at http://www.packtpub.com. If you purchased this book elsewhere, you can visit http://www.packtpub.com/support and register to have the files e-mailed directly to you.

You can download the code files by following these steps:

1. Log in or register to our website using your e-mail address and password.
2. Hover the mouse pointer on the **SUPPORT** tab at the top.
3. Click on **Code Downloads & Errata**.
4. Enter the name of the book in the **Search** box.
5. Select the book for which you're looking to download the code files.
6. Choose from the drop-down menu where you purchased this book from.
7. Click on **Code Download**.

You can also download the code files by clicking on the **Code Files** button on the book's webpage at the Packt Publishing website. This page can be accessed by entering the book's name in the **Search** box. Please note that you need to be logged in to your Packt account.

Once the file is downloaded, please make sure that you unzip or extract the folder using the latest version of:

- WinRAR / 7-Zip for Windows
- Zipeg / iZip / UnRarX for Mac
- 7-Zip / PeaZip for Linux

The code bundle for the book is also hosted on GitHub at `https://github.com/PacktPublishing/Learning-SaltStack-Second-Edition`. We also have other code bundles from our rich catalog of books and videos available at `https://github.com/PacktPublishing/`. Check them out!

Errata

Although we have taken every care to ensure the accuracy of our content, mistakes do happen. If you find a mistake in one of our books—maybe a mistake in the text or the code—we would be grateful if you could report this to us. By doing so, you can save other readers from frustration and help us improve subsequent versions of this book. If you find any errata, please report them by visiting `http://www.packtpub.com/submit-errata`, selecting your book, clicking on the **Errata Submission Form** link, and entering the details of your errata. Once your errata are verified, your submission will be accepted and the errata will be uploaded to our website or added to any list of existing errata under the Errata section of that title.

To view the previously submitted errata, go to `https://www.packtpub.com/books/content/support` and enter the name of the book in the search field. The required information will appear under the **Errata** section.

Piracy

Piracy of copyrighted material on the Internet is an ongoing problem across all media. At Packt, we take the protection of our copyright and licenses very seriously. If you come across any illegal copies of our works in any form on the Internet, please provide us with the location address or website name immediately so that we can pursue a remedy.

Please contact us at `copyright@packtpub.com` with a link to the suspected pirated material.

We appreciate your help in protecting our authors and our ability to bring you valuable content.

Questions

If you have a problem with any aspect of this book, you can contact us at `questions@packtpub.com`, and we will do our best to address the problem.

1
Diving In – Our First Salt Commands

Salt is more than just configuration management or remote execution. It is a powerful platform that not only gives you unique tools to manage your infrastructure, but also the power to create new tools to fit your infrastructure's unique needs. However, everything starts with the foundation of lightning-fast remote execution, so that's where we will start.

In this chapter, you will learn how to:

- Install Salt
- Configure the master and the minion
- Connect the minion to the master
- Run our first remote execution commands

This book assumes that you already have root access on a device with a common distribution of Linux installed. The machine used in the examples in this book is running Ubuntu 14.04, unless otherwise stated. Most examples should run on other major distributions, such as recent versions of Fedora, RHEL 6/7, or Arch Linux.

Introducing Salt

Before installing Salt, we should learn the basic architecture of Salt deployment.

The two main pieces of Salt are the **Salt master** and the **Salt minion**. The master is the central hub. All minions connect to the master to receive instructions. From the master, you can run commands and apply configuration across hundreds or thousands of minions in seconds.

The minion, as mentioned earlier, connects to the master and treats the master as the source of all truth. Although minions can exist without a master, the full power of Salt is realized when you have minions and the master working together.

Salt is built on two major concepts: **remote execution** and **configuration management**. In the remote execution system, Salt leverages Python to accomplish complex tasks with single-function calls. The configuration management system in Salt, **States**, builds upon the remote execution foundation to create repeatable, enforceable configuration for the minions.

With this bird's-eye view in mind, let's get Salt installed so that we can start learning how to use it to make managing our infrastructure easier!

Installing Salt

The dependencies for running Salt at the time of writing are as follows:

- Python 2 – Version 2.6 or greater (Salt is not Python 3-compatible)
- Msgpack – python
- YAML
- Jinja2
- MarkupSafe
- ZeroMQ – Version 3.2.0 or greater
- PyZMQ – Version 2.2.0 or greater
- Tornado
- PyCrypto
- M2Crypto

The easiest way to ensure that the dependencies for Salt are met is to use system-specific package management systems, such as `apt` on Ubuntu systems, that will handle the dependency-resolution automatically. You can also use the Salt Bootstrap script to handle all of the system-specific commands for you. **Salt Bootstrap** is an open source project with the goal of creating a Bourne shell-compatible script that will install Salt on any compatible server. The project is managed and hosted by the SaltStack team. You can find more information at `https://github.com/saltstack/salt-bootstrap`.

We will explore each of these methods of installation in turn, on a few different platforms.

Installation with system packages (Ubuntu)

The latest release of Salt for Ubuntu is provided via the official SaltStack package repository at http://repo.saltstack.com.

First, you must add the official SaltStack GPG key so that the packages can be verified:

```
# wget -O - https://repo.saltstack.com/apt/ubuntu/14.04/amd64/latest/
SALTSTACK-GPG-KEY.pub | sudo apt-key add -
```

Now, you must open the file /etc/apt/sources.list and add the following line:

```
deb http://repo.saltstack.com/apt/ubuntu/14.04/amd64/latest trusty main
```

Save and close that file.

After you have added the repository, you must update the package management database, as follows:

```
# sudo apt-get update
```

You should then be able to install the Salt master and the Salt minion with the following command:

```
# sudo apt-get install salt-master salt-minion
```

Assuming there are no errors after running this command, you should be done! Salt is now installed on your machine.

Note that we have installed both the Salt master and the Salt minion. The term master refers to the central server—the server from which we will be controlling all of our other servers. The term minion refers to the servers connected to and controlled by a master.

Installation with system packages (CentOS 6)

The latest release of Salt for RedHat/CentOS systems is also provided via the official SaltStack package repository at http://repo.saltstack.com.

You can set up both the repository and the keys required with a single command:

```
# sudo rpm -ivh https://repo.saltstack.com/yum/redhat/salt-repo-
2015.8.el6.noarch.rpm
```

Make sure that the caches are clean with the following command:

```
# sudo yum clean expire-cache
```

Then, install the Salt master and Salt minion with the following commands:

```
# sudo yum install salt-master
# sudo yum install salt-minion
```

Assuming that there are no errors after running this command, you should be done! Salt is now installed on your machine.

As with Ubuntu, we installed both the Salt master and the Salt minion. The term master refers to the central server — the server from which we will be controlling all of our other servers. The term minion refers to the servers connected to and controlled by a master.

Installation with system packages (Windows)

The latest release of Salt for Windows systems is also provided via official packages from SaltStack. However, because Windows doesn't currently have a built-in package manager, the process is more manual. You download the installer and then run it like you would install most other software on Windows.

Start by going to the Windows section of the SaltStack repo: http://repo.saltstack.com/#windows.

Here, you'll see links to the x86 and AMD64 versions of the Salt minion for Windows:

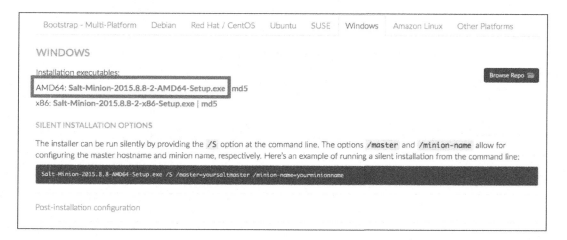

For most setups, you'll want the 64-bit version, highlighted in the preceding image. When you download and run that file, you'll see the following screen:

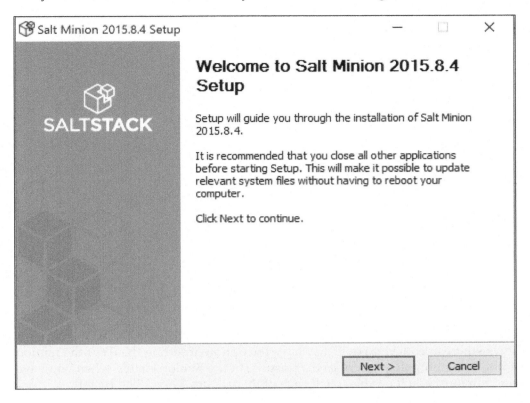

Continue the installation process by clicking **Next** and agreeing to the license agreement.

You'll then be shown a configuration page:

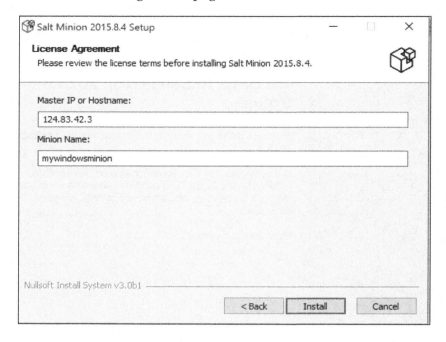

Here, you can enter the hostname or IP address of your Salt master, so the minion knows where to connect. You'll also have the option of setting the ID of the minion. Set it to something that describes the purpose of the minion so that when you have many minions, you'll be able to tell each of them apart. Then, click **Install**.

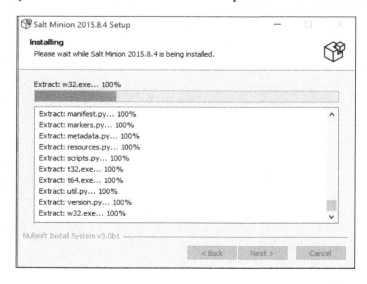

Once the installation completes, you'll have the option of starting the minion. Leave this box checked and click **Finish**:

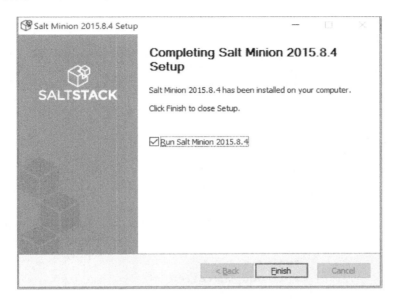

You are done! Salt is now installed on your machine.

Note that the Salt master is not supported on Windows machines, so we only installed the Salt minion on this machine.

Installing with Salt Bootstrap

Information about manual installation on other major Linux distributions can be found online at http://docs.saltstack.com. However, in most cases, it is easier and more straightforward to use the **Salt Bootstrap** script. In-depth documentation can be found on the project page at https://github.com/saltstack/salt-bootstrap; however, the tool is actually quite easy to use, as follows:

```
# curl -L https://bootstrap.saltstack.com -o install_salt.sh
# sudo sh install_salt.sh -h
```

We won't include the help text for Salt Bootstrap here as it would take up too much space. However, it should be noted that, by default, Salt Bootstrap will only install the Salt minion. We want both the Salt minion and the Salt master, which can be accomplished by passing in the -M flag. We also want to pass in the -P flag to allow bootstrap to install Tornado using pip:

```
# sudo sh install_salt.sh -M -P
```

The preceding command will result in a fully functional installation of Salt on your machine! The supported operating system list is extensive, as shown in the salt-bootstrap documentation at `https://github.com/saltstack/salt-bootstrap`.

The version of Salt used for the examples in this book is the 2015.8 release. Here is the full version information:

```
# sudo salt --versions-report
Salt Version:
          Salt: 2015.8.5

Dependency Versions:
          Jinja2: 2.7.2
          M2Crypto: Not Installed
          Mako: 0.9.1
          PyYAML: 3.10
          PyZMQ: 14.0.1
          Python: 2.7.6 (default, Mar 22 2014, 22:59:56)
          RAET: Not Installed
          Tornado: 4.2.1
          ZMQ: 4.0.4
          cffi: Not Installed
          cherrypy: Not Installed
          dateutil: 1.5
          gitdb: 0.5.4
          gitpython: 0.3.2 RC1
          ioflo: Not Installed
          libgit2: Not Installed
          libnacl: Not Installed
     msgpack-pure: Not Installed
   msgpack-python: 0.3.0
     mysql-python: 1.2.3
          pycparser: Not Installed
          pycrypto: 2.6.1
          pygit2: Not Installed
     python-gnupg: Not Installed
          smmap: 0.8.2
          timelib: Not Installed

System Versions:
          dist: Ubuntu 14.04 trusty
          machine: x86_64
          release: 3.13.0-46-generic
          system: Ubuntu 14.04 trusty
```

It's probable that the version of Salt you installed is a newer release and might have slightly different output. However, the examples should still all work in the latest version of Salt.

Configuring Salt

Now that we have the master and the minion installed on our machine, we must do a couple of pieces of configuration in order to allow them to talk to each other. From here on out, we're back to using a single Ubuntu 14.04 machine with both master and minion installed on the machine.

Firewall configuration

Since minions connect to masters, the only firewall configuration that must be done is on the master. By default, ports 4505 and 4506 must be able to accept incoming connections on the master. The default install of Ubuntu 14.04, used for these examples, actually requires no out-of-the-box firewall configuration to be able to run Salt; the ports required are already open. However, many distributions of Linux come with much more restrictive default firewall settings. The most common firewall software in use on Linux systems is **iptables**.

 Note that you might also have to change firewall settings on your network hardware if there is network filtering in place outside the software on the machine on which you're working.

Firewall configuration is a topic that deserves its own book. However, our needs for the configuration of Salt are fairly simple. First, you must find the set of rules currently in effect for your system. This varies from system to system; for example, the file is located in /etc/sysconfig/iptables on RedHat distributions, while it is located at /etc/iptables/iptables.rules in Arch Linux.

Once you find that file, add the following lines to that file, but be sure to do it above the line that says DROP:

```
-A INPUT -m state --state new -m tcp -p tcp --dport 4505 -j ACCEPT
-A INPUT -m state --state new -m tcp -p tcp --dport 4506 -j ACCEPT
```

For more information about configuring on your operating system of choice so that your Salt minion can connect successfully to your Salt master, see the Salt documentation at http://docs.saltstack.com/en/latest/topics/tutorials/firewall.html.

Salt minion configuration

Out of the box, the Salt minion is configured to connect to a master at the location salt. The reason for this default is that, if DNS is configured correctly such that salt resolves to the master's IP address, no further configuration is needed. The minion will connect successfully to the master.

However, in our example, we do not have any DNS configuration in place, so we must configure it ourselves.

The minion and master configuration files are located in the /etc/salt/ directory.

The /etc/salt/ directory should be created as part of the installation of Salt, assuming that you followed the preceding directions. If it does not exist for some reason, please create the directory and create two files, minion and master, within the directory.

Open the /etc/salt/minion file with your text editor of choice (remember to use the sudo command!). We will be making a couple of changes to this file.

First, find the commented-out line for the configuration option master. It should look like this:

```
#master:    salt
```

Uncomment that line and change salt to localhost (as we have this minion connected to the local master). It should look like this:

```
master: localhost
```

If you cannot find the appropriate line in the file, just add the line shown previously to the top of the file.

You should also manually configure the minion ID so that you can more easily follow along with the examples in this text. Find the ID line:

```
#id:
```

Uncomment it and set it to myminion:

```
id: myminion
```

Again, if you cannot find the appropriate line in the file, just add the line shown previously to the top of the file.

Save and close the file.

 Without a manually specified minion ID, the minion will try to intelligently guess what its minion ID should be at startup. For most systems, this will mean that the minion ID will be set to the **Fully Qualified Domain Name (FQDN)** for the system.

Starting the Salt master and Salt minion

Now we need to start (or restart) our Salt master and Salt minion. Assuming that you're following along on Ubuntu (which I recommend), you can use the following commands:

```
# sudo service salt-minion restart
# sudo service salt-master restart
```

Packages in other supported distributions ship with `init` scripts for Salt. Use whichever service system is available to you to start or restart the Salt minion and Salt master.

Accepting the minion key on the master

There is one last step remaining before we can run our first Salt commands. We must tell the master that it can trust the minion. To help us with this, Salt comes with the `salt-key` command to help us manage minion keys:

```
# sudo salt-key
Accepted Keys:
Denied Keys:
Unaccepted Keys:
myminion
Rejected Keys:
```

Note that our minion, myminion, is listed in the Unaccepted Keys section. This means that the minion has contacted the master and the master has cached that minion's public key, and is waiting for further instructions as to whether to accept the minion or not.

If your minion is not showing up in the output of salt-key, it's possible that the minion cannot reach the master on ports 4505 and 4506. Please refer to the *Firewall configuration* section described previously for more information.

Troubleshooting information can also be found in the Salt documentation at http://docs.saltstack.com/en/latest/topics/troubleshooting/.

We can inspect the key's fingerprint to ensure that it matches our minion's key, as follows:

```
# sudo salt-key -f myminion
Unaccepted Keys:
myminion:  a8:1f:b0:c2:ab:9d:27:13:60:c9:81:b1:11:a3:68:e1
```

We can use the salt-call command to run a command on the minion to obtain the minion's key, as follows:

```
# sudo salt-call --local key.finger
local:     a8:1f:b0:c2:ab:9d:27:13:60:c9:81:b1:11:a3:68:e1
```

Since the fingerprints match, we can accept the key on the master, as follows:

```
# sudo salt-key -a myminion
The following keys are going to be accepted:
Unaccepted Keys:
myminion
Proceed? [n/Y] Y
Key for minion myminion accepted.
```

We can check that the minion key was accepted, as follows:

```
# sudo salt-key
Accepted Keys:
myminion
Denied Keys:
Unaccepted Keys:
Rejected Keys:
```

Success! We are ready to run our first Salt command!

A game of ping pong

Here's our first command:

```
# sudo salt '*' test.ping
myminion:
    True
```

Was that a bit underwhelming?

Don't worry. We're going to get to the more impressive stuff soon enough.
The command we just ran was a remote execution command. Basically, we sent
a message to all (one) of our minions and told them to run a function from one of
the execution modules that is built into Salt. In this case, we just told our minion to
return `True`. It's a good way to check which of our minions are alive. We will explore
the various parts of this command in more detail in the next chapter.

The `test` module actually has a few other useful functions. To find out about them,
we're actually going to use another module, `sys`, as follows:

```
# sudo salt 'myminion' sys.list_functions test
myminion:
    - test.arg
    - test.arg_repr
    - test.arg_type
    - test.collatz
    - test.conf_test
    - test.cross_test
    - test.echo
    - test.exception
    - test.fib
    - test.get_opts
    - test.kwarg
    - test.not_loaded
    - test.opts_pkg
    - test.outputter
    - test.ping
    - test.provider
    - test.providers
    - test.rand_sleep
```

- `test.rand_str`
- `test.retcode`
- `test.sleep`
- `test.stack`
- `test.tty`
- `test.version`
- `test.versions_information`
- `test.versions_report`

Let's try one of the other functions on the list, maybe `test.fib`:

```
# sudo salt '*' test.fib
```

```
myminion:
```

```
    Passed invalid arguments to test.fib: fib() takes exactly 1 argument
(0 given)
```

Well, that didn't work. To find out more information about a function, including examples of how to use it, we can use the `sys.doc` function, as follows:

```
# sudo salt '*' sys.doc test.fib
```

```
test.fib:
```

```
    Return a Fibonacci sequence up to the passed number, and the
    timeit took to compute in seconds. Used for performance tests
```

```
    CLI Example:
```

```
    salt '*' test.fib 3
```

In recent versions of salt, the docs for a function are returned along with the error by default. However, sys.doc is still useful for discovering docs even without errors, which is why this example is still relevant.

Aha! We need to give it a number to which it should calculate the fibonacci sequence, as follows:

```
# sudo salt '*' test.fib 30
```

```
myminion:
    |_
      - 0
```

```
        - 1
        - 1
        - 2
        - 3
        - 5
        - 8
        - 13
        - 21
    - 1.09672546387e-05
```

As it turns out, the fibonacci sequence is not very hard for computers to calculate quickly.

> Note that you can actually use sys.doc to retrieve the documentation for a whole module's worth of functions at a time, as follows:
>
> # sudo salt '*' sys.doc test
>
> I didn't include the output as it is lengthy.

The sys module is going to be one of the most useful modules in your quest to learn Salt. Keep it handy and turn to it any time you want to learn more about something you're working with. Remember that the sys module can target itself. The following code shows you how to use the sys module:

```
# sudo salt '*' sys.list_functions sys
myminion:
    - sys.argspec
    - sys.doc
    - sys.list_functions
    - sys.list_modules
    - sys.list_renderers
    - sys.list_returner_functions
    - sys.list_returners
    - sys.list_runner_functions
    - sys.list_runners
    - sys.list_state_functions
    - sys.list_state_modules
    - sys.reload_modules
```

- `sys.renderer_doc`

- `sys.returner_argspec`

- `sys.returner_doc`

- `sys.runner_argspec`

- `sys.runner_doc`

- `sys.state_argspec`

- `sys.state_doc`

We are going to discuss remote execution and the execution modules in much greater detail in the next chapter.

Masterless Salt

In this chapter, we've taken the time to set up Salt in a master-minion relationship. This will allow us to take advantage of all the power of Salt and scale to multiple minions easily later on. However, Salt is also designed so that a minion can run without a master.

We'll run through a few examples of how to run commands on a minion. This will also be useful even when we do have a master because if we're logged into a minion for some reason and want to run a command while we're there, we can do so using these same concepts.

To start, we'll leave our master running. The command used to run commands on the minion is `salt-call`, and it can take any of the same execution module functions that we used with the `salt` command, as follows:

```
# sudo salt-call test.ping
local:
    True
```

Note that it doesn't display our minion's ID because we're just running it locally:

```
# sudo salt-call test.fib 10
local:
    |_
      - 0
      - 1
      - 1
      - 2
      - 3
```

```
    - 5
    - 8
- 5.00679016113e-06
# sudo salt-call sys.doc test.ping
local:
    ----------
    test.ping:

            Used to make sure the minion is up and responding. Not
            an ICMP ping.

            Returns ``True``.

            CLI Example:

                salt '*' test.ping
```

Now, let's stop our master and try again:

```
# sudo service salt-master stop
# sudo salt-call test.ping
Failed sign in
```

The example shown previously will take a fairly long time to terminate. Basically, salt-call is trying to establish a connection with the master just in case it needs to copy files from the master or other similar operations.

In order for salt-call to operate properly without a master, we need to tell it that there's no master. We do this with the --local flag, as follows:

```
# sudo salt-call --local test.ping
local:
    True
```

Success! You can now operate a Salt minion without a master!

 Start your master again before moving on to the next chapter of this book:
```
# sudo service salt-master start
```

Summary

We covered a lot of ground in this chapter. We installed the Salt minion and Salt master on our machines and configured them to talk to each other, including accepting the minion's key on the master. We also ran our first Salt commands, both from the master and from the minion without involving the master.

However, we've only just begun! In the next chapter, we're going to go much more in depth into the topic of remote execution and show how powerful this tool is.

2
Controlling Your Minions with Remote Execution

In the previous chapter, we installed our Salt minion and Salt master and learned how to send our first commands. We're ready to control all the systems in our infrastructure from a central server, our Salt master.

In this chapter, we are going to expand upon what we discussed there. You will learn the following:

- How a remote execution command is structured
- How to target minions in various ways
- Grains and how they are useful for remote execution
- The basic relationship between minion and master
- Practical examples of how you can use remote execution to make managing your servers easier

Let's get started!

The structure of a remote execution command

If you remember, our basic remote execution command looks like this:

```
# sudo salt '*' test.ping
myminion:
    True
```

The basic Salt remote execution command is made up of five distinct pieces. We can easily see them if we look at the usage text for the `salt` command, which is as follows:

```
# sudo salt --help
Usage: salt [options] '<target>' <function> [arguments]
```

Let's inspect a command that uses all of these pieces:

```
# sudo salt --verbose '*' test.sleep 2
Executing job with jid 20160218032023792688
-------------------------------------------

myminion:
    True
```

Here are the pieces of a Salt command, including the relevant pieces of the last command that we ran:

- The Salt command: `salt`
- Command-line options: `--verbose`
- Targeting string: `'*'`
- The Salt module function: `test.sleep`
- Arguments to the remote execution function: `2`

Let's briefly explore the purpose that each of these pieces serves.

Command-line options

If you've spent any real amount of time on the command line in Linux, you're probably very familiar with command-line options. They allow us to change the behavior of a program in various ways.

In Salt, there are a few main categories of command-line options.

Targeting options are used to target minions. We'll learn more about targeting minions later in the chapter.

Output options are also very useful. The information that minions return after a command is formed as basic data structures. This means that we can display it in different formats.

By default, most output is displayed via the `nested` outputter, as follows:

```
# sudo salt '*' cmd.run_all 'echo HELLO'
myminion:
    ----------
    pid:
        13999
    retcode:
        0
    stderr:

    stdout:
        HELLO
# sudo salt --out=nested '*' cmd.run_all 'echo HELLO'
myminion:
    ----------
    pid:
        14020
    retcode:
        0
    stderr:

    stdout:
        HELLO
```

You might note that we're using a new execution module in the preceding example. The `cmd` execution module is designed to provide ways to execute any commands or programs on the minions. You will see that `cmd.run_all` returns all the pieces of the return of that command as a dictionary, including `pid` of the command, the return code, the contents of `stdout`, and the contents of `stderr`. This particular command is a great example of how different types of data are displayed in the various outputters.

We can see the raw data with the `raw` outputter, as follows:

```
# sudo salt --out=raw '*' cmd.run_all 'echo HELLO'
{'myminion': {'pid': 14468, 'retcode': 0, 'stderr': '', 'stdout':
'HELLO'}}
```

For prettier output that still shows the data structures clearly, use the json outputter, as shown in the following code:

```
# sudo salt --out=json '*' cmd.run_all 'echo HELLO'
{
    "myminion": {
        "pid": 14506,
        "retcode": 0,
        "stderr": "",
        "stdout": "HELLO"
    }
}
```

You can also output it as YAML or just silence the output altogether using yaml or quiet, as we do in the following code:

```
# sudo salt --out=yaml '*' cmd.run_all 'echo HELLO'
myminion:
  pid: 14585
  retcode: 0
  stderr: ''
  stdout: HELLO
# sudo salt --out=quiet '*' cmd.run_all 'echo HELLO'
```

There are also options to disable or force colored output, or output the results of a Salt command to a file.

Miscellaneous options, such as --timeout, change the behavior of the Salt command in various ways. Here are a few of those options:

- --versions-report: This shows Salt's version and the versions of its dependencies (essential for bug reports).

- -t TIMEOUT **or** --timeout=TIMEOUT: This changes the initial timeout of the running command. This timeout is the amount of time the master will wait before checking to see whether any minions are still running the command. It is not a hard timeout for the job.

- --async: This runs a Salt command without waiting for the minions to respond with the results of the run. The minion will still run the job, but the results cannot be seen on the command line and must be retrieved from the job cache later using the provided job ID (jid).

- -v **or** --verbose: This turns on command verbosity — that is, it gives more information about what's happening with the command.

- --show-timeout: This shows which minions time out on a given command. This output is also shown with the --verbose command.

 Remember that you can always see the available command-line options by passing the --help option to a Salt command.

Targeting strings

In our examples until now, we've only been running a single minion. Salt actually does this really well, and some people even use Salt for a single minion to abstract away system administration tasks into easy-to-use modules.

However, it is much more common for Salt to be used to control many minions. Tens, hundreds, or even thousands of minions can be controlled by a single master. Instead of spending days logging in to each machine and running the same command, or even minutes or hours using an SSH loop, we can run the same command on thousands of machines in seconds.

However, we don't always want to run a command on all of our machines. Thus, we can target a subset of our machines using Salt's targeting system.

Glob matching

For every command that we've run until now, we've targeted '*':

```
# sudo salt '*' test.ping
myminion:
    True
```

This is using Salt's **glob** targeting. You're probably very familiar with glob. We use it all the time in fileserver operations, as shown in the following code:

```
# ls
1.txt  2.txt  3.txt  4.txt  5.txt
# rm *.txt
# ls
```

Note that, in the preceding example, we use a * to mean *anything*. So, we told the rm command that it should remove all files that have anything followed by .txt.

Globbing in Salt works in exactly the same way except that it matches on minion IDs, as follows:

```
# sudo salt '*' test.ping
myminion:
    True
# sudo salt '' test.ping
No minions matched the target.
# sudo salt 'myminion' test.ping
myminion:
    True
# sudo salt 'my*' test.ping
myminion:
    True
# sudo salt 'my*mini*' test.ping
myminion:
    True
# sudo salt 'larry' test.ping
No minions matched the target.
# sudo salt '*.txt' test.ping
No minions matched the target.
# sudo salt '??minion' test.ping
myminion:
    True
# sudo salt '[a-m]yminion' test.ping
myminion:
    True
```

Thus, by targeting *, we're telling Salt to target all of our minions.

Note that the previous examples demonstrate a variety of globbing syntaxes, which are well documented on Wikipedia and similar resources.

Globbing isn't the only targeting mechanism in Salt. In fact, there's a whole slew of available targeting mechanisms. You can see a list in the output of `salt --help`. We can use these alternative targeting mechanisms by passing in command-line flags to Salt. Let's explore some of these alternative targeting mechanisms.

Perl-compatible regular expression matching

If we need to perform more complex matches against the name of minions, we can use regular expressions. Salt uses the Python `re` library, which provides functions in order to parse **Perl-compatible regular expressions** (**PCRE**). If you're not familiar with the regular expressions, you can review the syntax on the Python website at `https://docs.python.org/2/library/re.html`.

PCRE matching requires an extra command-line option: `-E` or `--pcre`.

We can start off with a fairly simple example. Text in a PCRE string will be matched as shown in the following code:

```
# sudo salt -E 'myminion' test.ping
myminion:
    True
# sudo salt -E 'my' test.ping
myminion:
    True
```

 Note that, as shown in the second example, PCRE matching will accept a partial match, unlike globbing.

We can also simulate a * in globbing using the .* syntax, which means *any character, repeated zero or more times*, as shown in the following code:

```
# sudo salt -E '.*' test.ping
myminion:
    True
# sudo salt -E 'my.*n' test.ping
myminion:
    True
# sudo salt -E 'foo.*' test.ping
No minions matched the target.
```

If we want to eliminate partial matching, we can add anchors to the front and back of the targeting string (^ represents the beginning of the line, and $ matches the beginning of the line), as follows:

```
# sudo salt -E '^my$' test.ping
No minions matched the target.
# sudo salt -E '^myminion$' test.ping
myminion:
    True
```

We can also use the | (pipe) syntax for the *or* type of matches, where it will try to match A or B if we wrote A|B. We can use parentheses to group elements. This is encapsulated in the following code:

```
# sudo salt -E '((my)|(your))minion' test.ping
myminion:
    True
```

Question marks can be used to mark pieces of the target string as optional, as shown in the following code:

```
# sudo salt -E 'myminion(s)?' test.ping
myminion:
    True
# sudo salt -E '(my)?minion' test.ping
myminion:
    True
```

We've barely scratched the surface of what is possible with PCRE, but you now have the tools to do basic matches using PCRE. Remember to check the link given previously to the Python documentation for more information on regular expressions.

List matching

Sometimes, we just want to match a list of minions for a given command, without any fancy matching. This is easily possible using the list matcher. The list matcher is invoked with the -L or --list command-line option and takes a comma-separated list of minions, as shown in the following code:

```
# sudo salt -L 'myminion' test.ping
myminion:
    True
```

```
# sudo salt -L 'myminion,yourminion,theirminion' test.ping
myminion:
    True
# sudo salt -L 'anotherminion' test.ping
No minions matched the target.
```

Grain and pillar matching

Salt can also perform minion matches data in grains or pillars. **Grains** and **pillars** are two concepts specific to Salt. Both are key-value data stores where we can store data about, or for use by, our minions. We won't talk much about pillars until we get to the later chapter on states. However, know that both grains and pillars contain arbitrary data stored in the key-value format.

Using grains

Grains represent static data describing a minion. For example, minions have a grain named os_family, which describes the family of operating systems to which a minion belongs. For example, Ubuntu machines are a member of the Debian os_family. Here's how grains can be retrieved on the command line:

```
# sudo salt '*' grains.item os_family
myminion:
    ----------
    os_family:
        Debian
```

A Fedora or CentOS minion would be a member of the RedHat os_family.

If you want to know the exact type of operating system running on your minions, you can try the os grain or the osfinger grain:

```
# sudo salt '*' grains.item os
myminion:
    ----------
    os:
        Ubuntu
# sudo salt '*' grains.item osfinger
myminion:
    ----------
    osfinger:
        Ubuntu-14.04
```

Armed with this information, we can target just our Debian machines using the flag for targeting grains: `-G` or `--grain`:

```
# sudo salt --grain 'os_family:Debian' test.ping
myminion:
    True
```

Or we can target just our RedHat machines, as follows:

```
# sudo salt --grain 'os_family:RedHat' test.ping
No minions matched the target.
```

Or we could target more specifically—that is, perhaps just our Ubuntu machines:

```
# sudo salt -G 'os:Ubuntu' test.ping
myminion:
    True
# sudo salt -G 'os:ubuntu' test.ping
myminion:
    True
# sudo salt -G 'os:u*' test.ping
myminion:
    True
```

 Note that, as the second example here shows, grain matching is not case-sensitive and, as the third example shows, we can actually use glob matching in conjunction with grain matching.

However, we've only just brushed the surface of the information that is stored in grains. We can see a minion's whole list of grain data using the `grains.items` function, as follows:

```
# sudo salt '*' grains.items
myminion:
    ----------
    cpu_model:
        Intel(R) Xeon(R) CPU E5-2680 v2 @ 2.80GHz
    cpuarch:
        x86_64
    id:
```

```
    myminion
ipv4:
    - 127.0.0.1
    - 69.164.192.51
ipv6:
    - 2600:3c00::f03c:91ff:fe50:3f5d
    - ::1
    - fe80::f03c:91ff:fe50:3f5d
kernel:
    Linux
kernelrelease:
    3.15.4-x86_64-linode45
localhost:
    localhost
master:
    localhost
os:
    Ubuntu
os_family:
    Debian
osarch:
    amd64
oscodename:
    trusty
osfinger:
    Ubuntu-14.04
osfullname:
    Ubuntu
osrelease:
    14.04
ps:
    ps -efHww
saltpath:
    /usr/lib/python2.7/dist-packages/salt
saltversion:
    2014.7.0rc1
```

```
virtual:
    xen
virtual_subtype:
    Xen PV DomU
zmqversion:
    4.0.4
```

Note that, in the preceding output, I removed many values; otherwise, the output would have taken four to five pages. However, the output shows just how much information is encapsulated in the grain system. We can target any of these pieces of data when we do Salt remote execution. We can also use this data to make our configuration management (states) much more platform-agnostic, as we'll discover in a later chapter.

However, the fun with grains doesn't stop even here. We can set our own custom grains, as follows:

```
# sudo salt '*' grains.setval foo bar
salt myminion:
    ----------
    foo:
        bar
# sudo salt '*' grains.item foo
myminion:
    ----------
    foo:
        bar
```

We can use JSON syntax for more complex data structures, as shown in the following code:

```
# sudo salt '*' grains.setval baz '["larry", "moe", "curly"]'
myminion:
    ----------
    baz:
        - larry
        - moe
        - curly
# sudo salt '*' grains.item baz
myminion:
    ----------
    baz:
        - larry
        - moe
        - curly
```

Custom grains will persist, including across restarts of the master or the minion. We can get rid of unwanted custom grains in two ways: either by just deleting the value (grains.delval) or by deleting the key and value together (grains.delval with destructive=True), as the following code shows:

```
# sudo salt '*' grains.delval baz
myminion:
    None
# sudo salt '*' grains.item baz
myminion:
    ----------
    baz:
        None
# sudo salt '*' grains.delval baz destructive=True
myminion:
    None
# sudo salt '*' grains.item baz
myminion:
```

Note that, in the preceding grains.delval example, the return value of None is not particularly descriptive, but you can rest assure that the value has been deleted as we tested later with the grains.item call. The grains.item call also looks a little interesting. If we show the output of that command in JSON using the flag --out=json, we can see that an empty dictionary was returned for our minion, which results in the empty output we saw previously with the default nested outputter.

> Custom grain data is stored in a file on the minion. This file is managed by Salt, so manual changes will be lost.
>
> ```
> # cat /etc/salt/grains
> baz:
> - larry
> - moe
> - curly
> foo: bar
> ```

Using pillars

Pillar data is similar to grains, except that it can be defined more dynamically and is a secure store for data. We will talk more about the implications of this in *Chapter 5, Expanding Our States with Jinja2 and Pillar*. Just note that, since it is also a key-value store, you can match it just as with grains except that you use the -I or --pillar flag.

Compound matching

The last form of matching we will discuss in this book is perhaps the most powerful matching, that is, compound matching.

With compound matching, we are able to specify much more granular and complex matches of our minions, combining the targeting methods discussed previously as well as a few others that we don't cover in this book.

A compound match can look like this:

```
# sudo salt -C '*minion and G@os:Ubuntu and not L@yourminion,theirminion'
test.ping
myminion:
    True
```

Let's look at just the targeting string on its own, as follows:

```
'*minion and G@os:Ubuntu and not L@yourminion,theirminion'
```

Basically, the compound matcher combines a series of match strings using the Boolean operators and, or, and not between match strings. It also uses a letter and the @ symbol to specify the type of match for each section.

By default, match strings are matched using the default glob matching. Thus, the *minion part of the match specifies all minions that end with minion. As for the rest of the match types, here is a table, directly from the official Salt documentation (http://docs.saltstack.com/en/latest/topics/targeting/compound.html), that enumerates the possible match types and their associated letter:

Letter	Match type	Example
G	Grains glob	G@os:Ubuntu
E	PCRE minion ID	E@web\d+\.(dev|qa|prod)\.loc
P	Grains PCRE	P@os:(RedHat|Fedora|CentOS)
L	The list of minions	L@minion1.example.com, minion3.domain.com

Letter	Match type	Example
I	Pillar glob	`I@pdata:foobar`
S	Subnet/IP address	`S@192.168.1.0/24` or `S@192.168.1.100`
R	Range cluster	`R@%foo.bar`

Thus, the match that we used here can be summed up like this:

- Start with the minions whose IDs end in "minion" (those whose IDs match the glob pattern `*minion`)

- From the remaining minions, select those that are running Ubuntu (those that have the grain `os:Ubuntu`)

- From the remaining minions, select those that are not in the following list of minions:
  - `yourminion`
  - `theirminion`

Let's take another example. Say we wanted to target all of our minions that are not running RedHat. We could do something like this:

```
# sudo salt -C '* and not G@os_family:RedHat' test.ping
myminion:
    True
```

Again, we can follow this match through logically:

1. Start with all minions (those whose IDs match the glob pattern `*`)
2. From the remaining minions, select those that are not running a RedHat distribution of Linux (those that do not have the grain `os_family:RedHat`)

Finally, here's an example using the `or` operator:

```
# sudo salt -C 'G@os:Ubuntu or G@os:Fedora' test.ping
myminion:
    True
```

One more note on the compound matcher — you cannot use a leading `not` operator, as shown in the following example:

```
# sudo salt -C 'not G@os_family:redhat' test.ping
No minions matched the target.
```

Instead, you must start with a normal match (usually *) and then combine that with the not operator using and:

```
# sudo salt -C '* and not G@os_family:redhat' test.ping
myminion:
    True
```

 The examples of matching here are a bit contrived since we only have a single minion. However, hopefully, you have grasped the power of these various targeting methods when you have tens, hundreds, or even thousands of servers.

Remote execution modules and functions

The final piece of our remote execution command is the actual function that we want to run and arguments to this function (if there are any). These functions are separated into logical groupings named execution modules. For example, test is an execution module, inside which we find the function ping. All remote execution commands come in the format <module>.<function>.

We can obtain a list of all available execution modules using the sys module we used in *Chapter 1, Diving In – Our First Salt Commands*. Note that Salt ships with all available modules, so there is no need to install additional modules (unless you write your own, as we will see in *Chapter 3, Execution Modules – Write Your Own Solution*). Here's how we use the sys module:

```
# sudo salt '*' sys.list_modules
myminion:
    - aliases
    - alternatives
    - archive
    - at
    - blockdev
    - buildout
    - cloud
...
    - sys
    - sysctl
    - system
    - test
```

- `timezone`
- `tls`
- `user`
- `virtualenv`

I have abbreviated my output—yours should be longer.

We can also find a list of all modules and their complete documentation in the SaltStack online documentation, in the list of all modules at `http://docs.saltstack.com/en/latest/salt-modindex.html`. Here's a screenshot of that page:

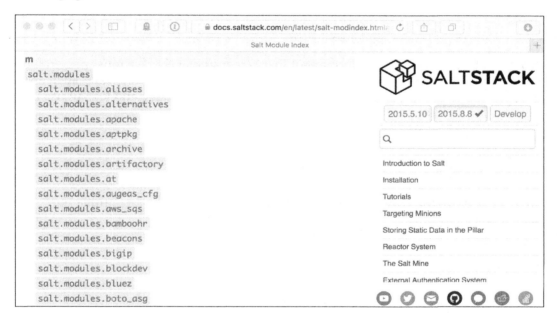

Make sure that you click on the **m** link at the top of the page or scroll down to the **salt.modules** section, as shown in the preceding screenshot. Note that there's a permanent link at the top of all Salt documentation pages that will bring you to this module index.

You'll note that there are execution modules that perform many varieties of tasks. There are routines to manage services, databases, packages, and users—if a task is common in system administration, it probably has an execution module available.

Let's learn about some of the common modules and run some examples.

Adding users

First up is user management—a task every system administrator has to deal with at some point. For this example, we will use the user.add function, as follows:

```
# sudo salt '*' sys.doc user.add
user.add:

    Add a user to the minion

    CLI Example:

        salt '*' user.add name <uid> <gid> <groups> <home> <shell>
```

Note that this module has one argument that is required: name. We must pass in the name of the user we want to add. In addition, we can pass in other details, such as uid, groups, or the home directory. For now, let's just add a user and let Salt use the defaults for the other settings, as follows:

```
# sudo salt '*' user.add larry
myminion:
    True
```

Now we can ask the minion about our new user using the user.info function, as follows:

```
# sudo salt '*' user.info larry
myminion:
    ----------
    fullname:

    gid:
        1000
    groups:
        - larry
    home:
        /home/larry
    homephone:

    name:
        larry
```

```
passwd:

    x

roomnumber:


shell:


uid:

    1000

workphone:
```

Success! We have a new user named larry!

Installing packages

Package installation and management are another important aspect of system administration. For this purpose, Salt provides the pkg module. We can use pkg.install to install packages, as follows:

```
# sudo salt '*' sys.doc pkg.install
pkg.install:

    Install the passed package, add refresh=True to update the dpkg
    database.
...
    CLI Example:

        salt '*' pkg.install <package name>
```

Again, I abbreviated the output as the documentation for this function is quite lengthy.

Let's install the package for the Apache web server. The package name we will use is apache2 (note that, if you're testing on a RedHat machine, you need to use the package name httpd instead), as follows:

```
# sudo salt '*' pkg.install apache2
myminion:
    ----------
    apache2:
        ----------
        new:
```

```
        2.4.7-1ubuntu4.1
    old:


apache2-api-20120211:
    ----------
    new:
        1
    old:


apache2-bin:
    ----------
    new:
        2.4.7-1ubuntu4.1
    old:


apache2-data:
    ----------
    new:
        2.4.7-1ubuntu4.1
    old:
```

Note that Salt shows us all of the package changes made, including dependencies.

We can also ask the minion about installed packages. We can get a list of all installed packages with pkg.list_pkgs, and we can ask about a specific package with pkg. version. The following commands show us how this is done:

```
# sudo salt '*' pkg.list_pkgs
myminion:
    ----------
    adduser:
        3.113+nmu3ubuntu3
    apache2:
        2.4.7-1ubuntu4.1
    apache2-api-20120211:
        1
    apache2-bin:
        2.4.7-1ubuntu4.1
```

```
    apache2-data:
        2.4.7-1ubuntu4.1
    apt:
        1.0.1ubuntu2.1
...
# sudo salt '*' pkg.version nano
myminion:
    2.2.6-1ubuntu1
```

We can also remove packages with `pkg.remove`:

```
# sudo salt '*' pkg.install htop
myminion:
    ----------
    htop:
        ----------
        new:
            1.0.2-3
        old:

# sudo salt '*' pkg.remove htop
myminion:
    ----------
    htop:
        ----------
        new:

        old:
            1.0.2-3
# sudo salt '*' pkg.version htop
myminion:
```

Note that the lack of output is because Salt actually returned an empty dictionary, which results in no output from the default `nested` outputter. If you want to know more explicitly the structure of the output from a Salt command, use the JSON outputter with the `--out=json` command-line option.

Salt adds an abstraction layer on top of certain module types. For example, Ubuntu machines running the pkg functions need to use apt, while RedHat machines need to use yum to install packages.

This is accomplished by setting up multiple execution modules to resolve to the same name: pkg. In the source code, examples of these modules are aptpkg.py, yumpkg.py, and pacman.py. We will talk more about this abstraction layer in the next chapter—for now, just know that your minion will use the correct pkg module automatically.

A similar abstraction layer is used for the user module, the service module, and the group module.

Managing services

Salt also allows us to easily manage services on our minions. We use the service module, with functions such as service.start, service.status, and service. stop, to name a few.

Here, we will use the apache2 service to demonstrate. If you followed the preceding pkg example, you should already have apache2 installed. (A note for RedHat users: you should use httpd instead of apache2). Note that a result of True from the service.status remote execution module function means the service is running, while a result of False means the service is stopped. When starting or stopping a service, a result of True means that the operation was successful:

```
# sudo salt '*' service.status apache2
myminion:
    True
# sudo salt '*' service.stop apache2
myminion:
    True
# sudo salt '*' service.status apache2
myminion:
    False
# sudo salt '*' service.start apache2
myminion:
    True
```

Monitoring minion states

In order to retrieve the status of our minions, we will use functions provided by the `status` module.

Let's start by checking on the disk usage of our minions to make sure that we have plenty of available disk space. We will use the function `status.diskusage`, as follows:

```
# sudo salt '*' status.diskusage
myminion:
    ----------
    /:
        ----------
        available:
            23927775232
        total:
            25034108928
    /dev:
        ----------
        available:
            518504448
        total:
            518508544
```

We can also check on the CPU usage. If we want many details on our CPU usage, we can use `status.cpustats`. However, in this case, we really only want to know the load average of our CPU; thus, we can use `status.loadavg`, as shown in the following example:

```
# sudo salt '*' status.loadavg
myminion:
    ----------
    1-min:
        0.07
    15-min:
        0.13
    5-min:
        0.09
```

Memory information is obtained using `status.meminfo`, as follows:

```
# sudo salt '*' status.meminfo
myminion:
    ----------
    Active:
        ----------
        unit:
            kB
        value:
            420796
    Active(anon):
        ----------
        unit:
            kB
        value:
            269900
```

Finally, uptime for our server can be obtained using `status.uptime`, as follows:

```
# sudo salt '*' status.uptime
myminion:
    22:41:58 up 12 days,  3:44,  1 user,  load average: 0.13, 0.10,
    0.13
```

Running arbitrary commands

To finish our discussion of remote execution modules, we will look at the `cmd` module. This module is designed to give us direct access to run commands or scripts on the minion.

The most basic function is `cmd.run`, which runs a command and returns its output, as shown in the following code:

```
# sudo salt '*' cmd.run 'echo Hello!'
myminion:
    Hello!
```

We also have commands to just return pieces of a command from the minion, such as `cmd.run_stderr`, `cmd.run_stdout`, and `cmd.retcode` (which return the STDERR, STDOUT, and return code for the command, respectively). The following examples show the difference between these functions:

```
# sudo salt '*' cmd.run_stdout 'echo Hello!'
myminion:
    Hello!
# sudo salt '*' cmd.run_stderr 'echo Hello!'
myminion:

# sudo salt '*' cmd.retcode 'echo Hello!'
myminion:
    0
```

If we want all of these pieces, but still split out separately, we can use `cmd.run_all`, as shown in the following example:

```
# sudo salt '*' cmd.run_all 'echo Hello!'
myminion:
    ----------
    pid:
        21243
    retcode:
        0
    stderr:

    stdout:
        Hello!
```

Also, note that each of these functions has arguments that allow us to run the command as a particular user, or in a particular directory, or in a particular shell. In addition, you can use the `cmd.script` function to run scripts stored in files.

Remember that whenever you see an execution module function in a Salt example or the documentation, you can see the documentation for the function using `sys.doc`.

Summary

In this chapter, we covered many aspects of remote execution, including the structure of a remote execution command in Salt. We also saw how to target minions based on a variety of data points, and you learned about the purpose of grains and how to use them in our targeting. Finally, you learned about common remote execution modules and how to use Salt to accomplish common tasks using these modules.

In the next chapter, you will learn more about how the code for execution modules is structured; we will even write our own custom execution module functions!

3
Execution Modules – Write Your Own Solution

In *Chapter 2, Controlling Your Minions with Remote Execution*, we went over remote execution commands in detail, learning how to target our commands and get things done using Salt's remote execution modules.

In this chapter, we will expand on Salt's remote execution system by diving into the code. You will learn the following things:

- What an execution module is made up of (and inspect some of the execution modules that ship with Salt)
- How to write our own execution module functions
- The extra tools that are easily available to us in the context of execution modules
- How to sync our execution modules to our minions

Note that in this chapter, we will be inspecting and writing a good deal of Python code. We will not be reviewing basic Python syntax, so if you're unfamiliar with Python, I recommend that you run through the tutorial at https://docs.python.org/2/tutorial/index.html or check out one of the many Python books available from Packt Publishing.

Exploring the source

By design, Salt makes it very easy to write your own custom execution modules and functions. It abstracts away much of the nitty-gritty about writing Python for system administration, yet leaves you with all the power of Python to get things done.

This means that we can write Salt modules that integrate with our own internal tools or proprietary software. We can even write quick modules just to reorganize or reformat data for use in other parts of Salt.

There will be more on that later. For now, let's inspect our first remote execution function in Salt, which is as follows:

```
def sleep(length):
    '''
    Instruct the minion to initiate a process that will sleep
    for a given period of time.

    CLI Example:

    .. code-block:: bash

        salt '*' test.sleep 20
    '''
    time.sleep(int(length))
    return True
```

This is the code for `test.sleep`, a function that we ran in the previous chapter. (Remember that execution modules take the form `<module>.<function>`, so this is the Python `sleep` function from the execution `test` module.) You can find this code yourself. Either clone Salt Git Repository yourself or navigate to the repository on GitHub at `https://github.com/saltstack/salt`, and then navigate to the `salt/modules/test.py` file.

This particular function is one of the most simple in Salt's library of execution modules. Note that the function, named `sleep`, takes one argument (the length of the sleep). Below the function declaration is a Python multiline string (delimited by triple quotes), which is named the docstring. Salt uses these docstrings to compile documentation for its various pieces. Docstrings should be written in **ReStructured Text (RST)**. We can see the result of this documentation compilation by going to the documentation for the test module at `http://docs.saltstack.com/en/latest/ref/modules/all/salt.modules.test.html#salt.modules.test.sleep`.

In the last two lines of the preceding code, we see the actual code that makes up the function. We use the `time` module from the Python standard library and `sleep` for `<length>` seconds. Then, we return `True`.

Let's look at another example from the `test` module, which actually does work,
`test.fib`:

```python
def fib(num):
    '''
    Return a Fibonacci sequence up to the passed number, and
    the time it took to compute in seconds. Used for
    performance tests

    CLI Example:

    .. code-block:: bash

        salt '*' test.fib 3
    '''
    num = int(num)
    start = time.time()
    fib_a, fib_b = 0, 1
    ret = [0]
    while fib_b < num:
        ret.append(fib_b)
        fib_a, fib_b = fib_b, fib_a + fib_b
    return ret, time.time() - start
```

Here, we see the same basic structure as in the `test.sleep` function. In this case, the
function once again takes a single argument and has a docstring. However, now we
see Python code that actually computes the Fibonacci sequence up to num, storing the
results in a list and then returning that list and the elapsed time. A summary of the
output for the preceding code is as follows:

```
# sudo salt '*' test.fib 10 --out=json
{
    "myminion": [
        [
            0,
            1,
            1,
            2,
            3,
            5,
            8
        ],
        1.6927719116210938e-05
    ]
}
```

From these examples, it's easy to see that there's nothing really unique about Salt execution module functions; they're just Python functions! However, we have some pretty cool tools to work with, provided for us by Salt.

Cross-calling execution modules

The first tool that Salt provides us with is the ability to cross-call execution module functions. When Salt loads all of the execution modules, it creates a dictionary with references to each execution module function. This dictionary is available as __salt__.

> Note that the double-underscore syntax, with two leading and two trailing underscores, (__salt__), is used in Python to represent a special variable. All special Salt references that are automatically made available in Salt code use this syntax.

We can see this dictionary in action in the pkg.refresh_db function, as follows:

```
def refresh_db():
    '''
    Updates the APT database to latest packages based upon
    repositories

    Returns a dict, with the keys being package databases and
    the values being the result of the update attempt. Values
    can be one of the following:

    - ``True``: Database updated successfully
    - ``False``: Problem updating database
    - ``None``: Database already up-to-date

    CLI Example:

    .. code-block:: bash

        salt '*' pkg.refresh_db
    '''
    ret = {}
    cmd = 'apt-get -q update'
```

```
    out = __salt__['cmd.run_stdout'](cmd, output_loglevel='trace')
for line in out.splitlines():
    cols = line.split()
    if not cols:
        continue
    ident = ' '.join(cols[1:])
    if 'Get' in cols[0]:
        # Strip filesize from end of line
        ident = re.sub(r' \[.+B\]$', '', ident)
        ret[ident] = True
    elif cols[0] == 'Ign':
        ret[ident] = False
    elif cols[0] == 'Hit':
        ret[ident] = None
return ret
```

On the third line of the body of the function, we can see the reference to __salt__:, which is provided again here for ease of reference:

```
    out = __salt__['cmd.run_stdout'](cmd, output_loglevel='trace')
```

This reference uses an execution module function we are already familiar with. Remember that cmd.run_stdout runs a shell command on the minion and returns the contents of STDOUT to us.

At this point, the power of __salt__ might have begun to dawn on you. Because we have access to all of Salt's other execution modules, we can take advantage of the convenience that they bring. Rather than having to use the subprocess Python module to create a separate process to run a shell command, we can just use cmd. run (or cmd.run_stdout in this case). We can write a function that installs packages (pkg.install), adds users (user.add), and restarts the system (system.reboot). As we write our own custom modules and functions, they get added to our __salt__ dictionary as well—ready for use. The possibilities are endless!

Remember that because we are on a Debian machine, our minion will automatically use the aptpkg.py module for its pkg functions. To see the preceding code in the source, navigate to salt/modules/aptpkg.py, as opposed to pkg.py. Let's discuss why that is and how that works.

Grains and the __virtual__ function

Near the top of our `aptpkg.py` file, we have some code I would like to draw your attention to:

```
# Define the module's virtual name
__virtualname__ = 'pkg'


def __virtual__():
    '''
    Confirm this module is on a Debian based system
    '''
    if __grains__.get('os_family', False) != 'Debian':
        return False
    return __virtualname__
```

As you look through the source for more of the execution modules, you might note that many execution modules contain code very similar to the previous code.

The `__virtual__` function is a function Salt looks for when it is loading execution modules. It serves a couple of purposes:

- It helps Salt decide whether to load the module
- It can rename the module if needed

In the case of `aptpkg.py`, it serves both these purposes. First, it uses `__grains__` (another dictionary provided by Salt, which gives access to your minion's grains values) to decide whether to load this module on this minion. Here's the code for your perusal:

```
    if __grains__.get('os_family', False) != 'Debian':
        return False
```

If the `__virtual__` function returns `False`, Salt will not load any functions from the module in question. In this case, we return `False` if the minion is running anything other than Debian.

Assuming that we pass the grains check, we hit the final line of the `__virtual__` function, which is as follows:

```
    return __virtualname__
```

Here, we return `__virtualname__`, which we can see is defined as the `'pkg'` string. Any string returned from this function will be used as the module name inside of Salt.

We learned that if we return a string from our __virtual__ function, then that string will be used as the module name. If we instead return True from a __virtual__ function, then Salt will load that module under its filename. We can see an example of this in the mysql module at salt/modules/mysql.py:, as follows:

```
# Import third party libs
try:
    import MySQLdb
    import MySQLdb.cursors
    import MySQLdb.converters
    from MySQLdb.constants import FIELD_TYPE, FLAG
    HAS_MYSQLDB = True
except ImportError:
    HAS_MYSQLDB = False


...


def __virtual__():
    '''
    Only load this module if the mysql libraries exist
    '''
    if HAS_MYSQLDB:
        return True
    return False
```

Note that this module only returns True if the required libraries are installed, and returns False otherwise. If False is returned, the module will not load at all. This is a common pattern in Salt.

Let's inspect one of the other pkg modules to compare its structure. This example is from yumpkg.py (salt/modules/yumpkg.py):

```
# Define the module's virtual name
__virtualname__ = 'pkg'

def __virtual__():
    '''
    Confine this module to yum based systems
    '''
    if __opts__.get('yum_provider') == 'yumpkg_api':
        return False
    try:
        os_grain = __grains__['os'].lower()
        os_family = __grains__['os_family'].lower()
```

```
        except Exception:
            return False


    enabled = ('amazon', 'xcp', 'xenserver')


    if os_family == 'redhat' or os_grain in enabled:
        return __virtualname__
    return False
```

This example might look more complex, but yumpkg.py itself must serve many more distributions, so the detection code has more checks as a result. We can see the same basic patterns in yumpkg.py that we saw in aptpkg.py—we return __virtualname__ ('pkg') if we decide that we want to load this module on our minion, and we return False otherwise.

Similar patterns hold true for modules that resolve to the __virtualname__ values service, group, and user. A full list of these modules is available in the Salt documentation at http://docs.saltstack.com/en/latest/ref/states/providers.html#provider-pkg.

The __opts__ and __pillar__ functions

You might have noted that there's another double underscore __<variable>__ in that last example. In addition to __grains__, __salt__, and __virtual__, Salt also provides us with two more dictionaries: __opts__ and __pillar__.

The first, __opts__, gives us the ability to access the minion configuration options in our execution modules. The interesting thing is that the minion options are not limited to those defaults defined inside the minion config file. In fact, we can store arbitrary keys and values inside the minion config file.

We still have not explored pillar data in depth. Remember that pillar is a secure storage for arbitrary data for minions. We will explore it in greater depth when we discuss states. However, it's useful to know at this point that we have access to this arbitrary data in our execution modules via the __pillar__ dictionary.

The MySQL module actually takes advantage of both these dictionaries. It requires you to set a few variables with the connection setting for the MySQL database. Here is an excerpt from salt/modules/mysql.py:

```
    prefix = 'connection_'
    if name.startswith(prefix):
        try:
            name = name[len(prefix):]
        except IndexError:
```

```
        return
val = __salt__['config.option']('mysql.{0}'.format(name), None)
if val is not None:
    connargs[key] = val
```

A large amount of context was left out of this snippet for brevity as we're really only interested in a small piece of the code. Here, the MySQL module is working to compile a series of arguments required to connect to a MySQL database. It will be looking for values inside the `minion config` and `master config` files, or pillar data. An example of the data for which it is looking is a key named `mysql.connection_host`, which will contain the host for the MySQL connection.

This is the important line:

```
val = __salt__['config.option']('mysql.{0}'.format(name), None)
```

Here, the MySQL module calls out to another execution module to do the search for it. Let's look at the `config.option` module it calls from `salt/modules/config.py`:

```python
def option(value,
           default='',
           omit_opts=False,
           omit_master=False,
           omit_pillar=False):
    '''
    Pass in a generic option and receive the value that will be
    assigned

    CLI Example:

    .. code-block:: bash

        salt '*' config.option redis.host
    '''
    if not omit_opts:
        if value in __opts__:
            return __opts__[value]
    if not omit_master:
        if value in __pillar__.get('master', {}):
            salt.utils.warn_until(
                'Lithium',
                'pillar_opts will default to False in the '
                'Lithium release'
            )
            return __pillar__['master'][value]
    if not omit_pillar:
```

```
        if value in __pillar__:
            return __pillar__[value]
    if value in DEFAULTS:
        return DEFAULTS[value]
    return default
```

Here, we can see that the `config.option` function will first search the minion options `__opts__`, then the master opts, which the minion has as part of its pillar data (`__pillar__.get('master')`), and finally the general store of pillar data (`__pillar__`) for the data in question. It also provides a way to define a default value just in case the data is undefined in any of these locations.

Now that we're aware of the available tools, let's create our first custom execution module function!

Reformatting return data

Let's come up with a simple use case. Let's say that we have an internal tool on our master. It needs a list of the users on each of our minions. We know that we can get such a list using the `user.list_users` function, which is shown in the following code:

```
# sudo salt '*' user.list_users
myminion:
    - backup
    - bin
    - daemon
    - games
    - gnats
    - irc
    - larry
    - libuuid
    - list
    - lp
    - mail
    - man
    - messagebus
    - news
    - nobody
    - ntp
```

- proxy
- root
- sshd
- sync
- sys
- syslog
- uucp
- www-data

However, our tool actually needs this list formatted as comma-separated values, instead of the list format provided by Salt. This is a perfect task for a simple custom module.

By default, our custom modules live in the /srv/salt/_modules/ folder, which is not created by default. Let's create it and create a new file inside the folder named customuser.py, as shown in the following code:

```
# sudo mkdir -p /srv/salt/_modules/
# sudo cd /srv/salt/_modules/
# sudo vim customuser.py
```

Here's the function we will put in that file:

```
def users_as_csv():
    '''
    Retrieve the users from a minion, formatted
    as comma-separated-values (CSV)

    CLI Example:

    .. code-block:: bash
        salt '*' customuser.users_as_csv
    '''
    user_list = __salt__['user.list_users']()
    csv_list = ','.join(user_list)
    return csv_list
```

We first retrieve the list of users using the same user.list_users function from before. Then, we join all the strings in that list using a comma as the separator. Finally, we return our new comma-separated list of users.

Now that we have our function written, it's time to sync it to all of our minions. We can use the `saltutil.sync_all` function for this purpose. Here's how we sync our function to all our minions:

```
# sudo salt '*' saltutil.sync_all
myminion:
    ----------
    grains:
    modules:
        - modules.customuser
    outputters:
    renderers:
    returners:
    states:
    utils:
```

Note that there is also a `saltutil.sync_modules` function, but we'd rather keep everything in sync, so we'll just use `saltutil.sync_all`.

Now that our minion has our custom module, let's test it! Here's how we will do it:

```
# sudo salt '*' customuser.users_as_csv
myminion:

backup,bin,daemon,games,gnats,irc,larry,libuuid,list,lp,mail,man,mess
agebus,news,nobody,ntp,proxy,root,sshd,sync,sys,syslog,uucp,www-data
```

Success! You have now successfully written your first custom execution module function!

But there's more. That execution module that we just synced is now a first-class citizen in our deployment. We can query the functions from that module using the following code:

```
# sudo salt '*' sys.list_functions customuser
myminion:
    - customuser.users_as_csv
```

We can also query the documentation for our new function in the following manner:

```
# sudo salt '*' sys.doc customuser.users_as_csv
customuser.users_as_csv:
```

```
Retrieve the users from a minion, formatted
as comma-separated-values (CSV)

CLI Example:

    salt '*' customuser.users_as_csv
```

Our custom module even shows up in the complete list of modules, as shown in the following output:

```
# sudo salt '*' sys.list_modules
myminion:
...
    - config
    - cp
    - cron
    - customuser
    - daemontools
    - data
    - debconf
...
```

Take the time to write documentation for your custom modules. You'll thank yourself in the future.

An advanced example

Remote execution modules are endlessly flexible. The tools are there, and you can write whatever you need to extend Salt to handle your infrastructure.

However, we're not going to try to explore every possible need your infrastructure might have, as that is impossible to do in the space allotted. Every environment is different, and we have explored the available tools well enough for you to be able to tackle those hurdles on your own.

Instead, we will explore a more complicated example of a remote execution module function from beginning to end and walk through the code.

The example that we will use is `file.replace`. This remote execution function is designed to replace text in a file based on a pattern. We can set arguments so that if a match is not found, it will prepend or append the text to the file. Here's a full list of arguments in the function declaration:

```
def replace(path,
            pattern,
            repl,
            count=0,
            flags=0,
            bufsize=1,
            append_if_not_found=False,
            prepend_if_not_found=False,
            not_found_content=None,
            backup='.bak',
            dry_run=False,
            search_only=False,
            show_changes=True,
            ):
```

We'll skip the docstring—if you're curious about the purpose of any of these arguments, remember that you can access the documentation for this function using the following command:

```
# sudo salt '*' sys.doc file.replace
```

As the first thing in the function, we do some basic checks to make sure that we even need to do work. We start with a check as to whether the file in question exists and make sure that it's a text file (as opposed to binary). We also do some argument checking. It doesn't make sense to have `search_only` set at the same time as the append or prepend options, and it doesn't make sense to set both of those arguments at the same time. The following is the code for the purposes outlined in this paragraph:

```
if not os.path.exists(path):
    raise SaltInvocationError('File not found: {0}'.format(path))

if not salt.utils.istextfile(path):
    raise SaltInvocationError(
        'Cannot perform string replacements on a binary file: {0}'
        .format(path)
    )
```

```
if search_only and (append_if_not_found or prepend_if_not_found):
    raise SaltInvocationError('Choose between search_only and '
    'append/prepend_if_not_found')

if append_if_not_found and prepend_if_not_found:
    raise SaltInvocationError('Choose between append or '
    'prepend_if_not_found')
```

Next, we're going to prepare the regular expression by compiling it (an optimization for later), obtaining the regular expression flags, making sure that the buffer size is set, and initializing some variables:

```
flags_num = _get_flags(flags)
cpattern = re.compile(pattern, flags_num)
if bufsize == 'file':
    bufsize = os.path.getsize(path)


# Search the file; track if any changes have been made for the
# return val
has_changes = False
orig_file = []  # used if show_changes
new_file = []  # used if show_changes
if not salt.utils.is_windows():
    pre_user = get_user(path)
    pre_group = get_group(path)
    pre_mode = __salt__['config.manage_mode'](get_mode(path))
```

Note that we call out to a `salt.utils.is_windows()` utility function—the `salt.utils` modules are also available to use in our execution module functions as well. These include basically any utility function that should be generally available in Salt, but that doesn't make sense for the utility function to be called from the command line.

Now we move on to the real work:

```
# Avoid TypeErrors by forcing repl to be a string
repl = str(repl)
try:
    fi_file = fileinput.input(path,
                    inplace=not dry_run,
                    backup=False if dry_run else backup,
                    bufsize=bufsize,
                    mode='rb')
    found = False
    for line in fi_file:
```

```
            if search_only:
                # Just search; bail as early as a match is found
                result = re.search(cpattern, line)

                if result:
                    return True
                    # `finally` block handles file closure
            else:
                result, nrepl = re.subn(cpattern, repl, line, count)

                # found anything? (even if no change)
                if nrepl > 0:
                    found = True

                # Identity check each potential change until one
                # change is made
                if has_changes is False and result is not line:
                    has_changes = True

                if show_changes:
                    orig_file.append(line)
                    new_file.append(result)

                if not dry_run:
                    print(result, end='', file=sys.stdout)
    finally:
        fi_file.close()
```

We first open the file to be read and then process it line by line (by default, this depends on buffer size). If we're only doing a search, we search each line until we find a match and then return the match. For the more common case of actually wanting to replace the pattern in the file, we use Python's regular expression library to do the actual substitution and keep track of the results so that we can show the diff of the file (if show_changes is True). Finally, after we're done looping over the file, we close the file.

We're still not quite done. We need to do some post-processing for our append or prepend arguments, and we need to actually overwrite the file with the changes we made if we're not doing a dry_run test. This is how we go about the task:

```
if not found and (append_if_not_found or prepend_if_not_found):
    if None == not_found_content:
        not_found_content = repl
```

```
        if prepend_if_not_found:
            new_file.insert(not_found_content + '\n')
        else:
            # append_if_not_found
            # Make sure we have a newline at the end of the file
            if 0 != len(new_file):
                if not new_file[-1].endswith('\n'):
                    new_file[-1] += '\n'
            new_file.append(not_found_content + '\n')
        has_changes = True
        if not dry_run:
            # backup already done in filter part
            # write new content in the file while avoiding partial
            # reads
            try:
                f = salt.utils.atomicfile.atomic_open(path, 'wb')
                for line in new_file:
                    f.write(line)
            finally:
                f.close()

    if not dry_run and not salt.utils.is_windows():
        check_perms(path, None, pre_user, pre_group, pre_mode)

    if show_changes:
        return ''.join(difflib.unified_diff(orig_file, new_file))

    return has_changes
```

We finish up by returning the diff file if show_changes is True, or just returning whether changes were made or not if show_changes is False.

Hopefully, this example has given you an idea of how you can use execution modules in your own infrastructure. Feel free to dive into other execution modules for more examples—the beauty of open source is that anyone can browse the source and use it for inspiration!

Summary

We covered a lot of material in this chapter. We looked at a number of examples of remote execution modules included in Salt and learned about the tools available to us as we write our own execution module functions. Finally, we created our own execution module, synced it to our minions, and ran it successfully!

In the next chapter, we're going to get into the configuration management aspect of Salt: *states*.

4

Defining the State of Your Infrastructure

In the previous chapter, we finished our deep dive of the remote execution system inside Salt. Remote execution is the foundation upon which all of the rest of Salt rests. In this chapter, you will learn about one of the most important systems: "the state system." You will learn the following:

- How states are structured and how to write our first state
- About the various pieces of the state declaration
- How to expand our state declarations to encompass multiple pieces of a state
- About ordering states with requisites

Our first state

Without further ado, let's write our first state. All Salt-specific files that aren't Python files end in the extension .sls. By default, the states are located in the /srv/salt/ directory. We created this directory in the previous chapter, but if you didn't follow along there, make this directory now, as follows:

```
# mkdir -p /srv/salt
# cd /srv/salt
```

Inside this directory, let's create a file named apache.sls, as shown in the following line of code:

```
# vim apache.sls
```

Here are the contents of that file:

```
install_apache:
  pkg.installed:
    - name: apache2
```

 State files are formatted using **Yet Another Markup Language (YAML)**. The most common syntax errors in state files are forgetting the colons at the end of the first two lines, so watch out for that. More information about YAML can be found at http://www.yaml.org/. In addition, many simple YAML parsers can be found with a simple Google search. These can be very useful to detect simple syntax errors.

Let's run our state. To apply states to our minions, we actually use the state execution module. For now, we will use the `state.sls` function, which allows us to run a single state file, as encapsulated by the following output:

```
# sudo salt '*' state.sls apache
myminion:
----------
          ID: install_apache
    Function: pkg.installed
        Name: apache2
      Result: True
     Comment: Package apache2 is already installed.
     Started: 20:21:00.498735
    Duration: 750.402 ms
     Changes:

Summary
------------
Succeeded: 1
Failed:    0
------------
Total states run:     1
```

Note that in *Chapter 2, Controlling Your Minions with Remote Execution*, we installed apache2 as part of our exploration of the `pkg` execution module. Thus, the `pkg.installed` state function tells us that the package is already installed and returns promptly.

If we remove the `apache2` package, we can see the behavior when we're installing a new package, which is shown in the following command lines (output summary):

```
# sudo salt '*' pkg.remove apache2
myminion:
    ----------
    apache2:
        ----------
        new:

        old:
            2.4.7-1ubuntu4.1
# sudo salt '*' state.sls apache
myminion:
----------
          ID: install_apache
    Function: pkg.installed
        Name: apache2
      Result: True
     Comment: The following packages were installed/updated: apache2.
     Started: 20:53:30.187526
    Duration: 10185.321 ms
     Changes:
              ----------
              apache2:
                  ----------
                  new:
                      2.4.7-1ubuntu4.1
                  old:


Summary
-----------
Succeeded: 1 (changed=1)
Failed:    0
-----------
Total states run:      1
```

If we were to run the state one more time, we would see the same results as our first run.

This highlights a major change between execution modules and state modules. Execution modules are iterative, whereas state modules are declarative. What do we mean by this? Execution module functions perform a task. In general, when you call the same execution module multiple times in succession, it will run the same logic and commands under the hood each time.

State module functions, on the other hand, are designed to be idempotent. An idempotent operation is one that only changes the result the first time it is applied. Subsequent applications do not continue to apply changes. Idempotent state modules functions are designed to do only as much work as necessary to create a given state on the target minion.

In the case of our first state, we are running a state module function, `pkg.installed`. Note the language change from execution modules. `pkg.install` tells the minion to "install this package." On the other hand, `pkg.installed` tells the minion to "ensure that this package is installed." Under the hood, `pkg.install` is just running `apt-get install <package>`, whereas `pkg.installed` actually calls out to the `pkg` execution module to find out whether the package is installed and only installs it if there's a need. It does the minimum amount of work to bring your minion into the correct state, nothing more.

We can access the documentation for state modules in the same ways as we can for execution modules.

We list the functions for a given state module with `sys.list_state_functions`, as follows:

```
# sudo salt '*' sys.list_state_functions pkg
myminion:
    - pkg.installed
    - pkg.latest
    - pkg.mod_aggregate
    - pkg.mod_init
    - pkg.purged
    - pkg.removed
    - pkg.uptodate
```

We can look up the documentation for a state module function using
`sys.state_doc`, as follows:

```
# sudo salt '*' sys.state_doc pkg.removed
myminion:
    ----------
    pkg:

        Installation of packages using OS package managers such as
        yum or apt-get

        ============================================================

        Salt can manage software packages via the pkg state module,
        packages can be set up to be installed, latest, removed and
        purged. Package management declarations are typically rather
        simple:

            vim:
              pkg.installed


        A more involved example involves pulling from a custom
        repository.  Note that the pkgrepo has a require_in clause.
        This is necessary and can not be replaced by a require clause
        in the pkg.

            base:
              pkgrepo.managed:
                - humanname: Logstash PPA
                - name: ppa:wolfnet/logstash
                - dist: precise
                - file: /etc/apt/sources.list.d/logstash.list
                - keyid: 28B04E4A
                - keyserver: keyserver.ubuntu.com
                - require_in:
                  - pkg: logstash
```

```
        logstash:
          pkg.installed


  pkg.removed:


        Verify that a package is not installed, calling
        ``pkg.remove`` if necessary to remove the package.
        name
            The name of the package to be removed.



        Multiple Package Options:


        pkgs

            A list of packages to remove. Must be passed as a
            python list.  The ``name`` parameter will be ignored
            if this option is passed.


        New in version 0.16.0
```

The pieces of a state declaration

Just as with our remote execution commands, state declarations can be broken up into multiple pieces. Here is our state from before:

```
install_apache:
  pkg.installed:
    - name: apache2
```

Here is information about how the pieces line up and what each piece of the state declaration is called:

```
<ID Declaration>:
  <State Module>.<Function>:
    - name: <name>
    - <Function Arg>
    - <Function Arg>
    - <Function Arg>
    - <Requisite Declaration>:
      - <Requisite Reference>
```

The preceding reference and more advanced examples can be found in the Salt documentation at `http://docs.saltstack.com/en/latest/ref/states/highstate.html#large-example`.

We haven't talked about requisites yet, so ignore that section for the moment.

We start with the ID of our state. This is a string that must be unique across all of the states we are running at a given time. Note that it doesn't have to follow stringent requirements like a variable in a programming language—it can contain letters, numbers, spaces, and underscores—but just needs to be a valid Python string. You should always try to keep it simple and descriptive.

Finally, we have our function arguments. The first argument is always `name`, followed by any additional arguments required for the state.

Expanding to encompass multiple pieces of state

We now have our state declaration, which ensures that the `apache2` package is installed on each of our minions. However, `apache2` will not necessarily be running on our systems.

We know that we can start `apache2` using the `service.start` execution module function, as follows:

```
# sudo salt '*' service.status apache2
myminion:
    False
# sudo salt '*' service.start apache2
myminion:
    True
# sudo salt '*' service.status apache2
myminion:
    True
```

Really, we just want to make sure that `apache2` is running. Repeatedly running `service.start` does serve this purpose, but it's not very stateful. Instead, let's use the `service.running` state module function. Again, note the change in language—rather than starting the service (`service.start`), we're going to just ensure that it's running (`service.running`).

Let's first glance at the documentation for this function:

```
# sudo salt '*' sys.state_doc service.running
myminion:
    ----------
...
    service.running:

        Verify that the service is running

        name

            The name of the init or rc script used to manage the
            service

        enable

            Set the service to be enabled at boot time, True sets
            the service to be enabled, False sets the named
            service to be disabled. The default is None, which
            does not enable or disable anything.

        sig

            The string to search for when looking for the service
            process with ps
```

Note that this module has an `enable` argument, which we're going to use to make sure that `apache2` starts on boot on each of our minions. We're going to add a few lines to our `apache.sls` file from before:

```
install_apache:
  pkg.installed:
    - name: apache2

make sure apache is running:
  service.running:
    - name: apache2
    - enable: True
```

Note that in this example, I used *spaces* in my ID declaration. This is perfectly valid and is left to the preference of the user.

Let's apply our state again:

```
# sudo salt '*' state.sls apache
myminion:
----------
          ID: install_apache
    Function: pkg.installed
        Name: apache2
      Result: True
     Comment: Package apache2 is already installed.
     Started: 22:54:44.143934
    Duration: 718.254 ms
     Changes:
----------
          ID: make sure apache is running
    Function: service.running
        Name: apache2
      Result: True
     Comment: Service apache2 is already enabled, and is in the
     desired state
     Started: 22:54:44.862391
    Duration: 90.917 ms
     Changes:

Summary
------------
Succeeded: 2
Failed:    0
------------
Total states run:      2
```

Great, now we know that whenever we run our apache.sls state file, our minion will ensure that Apache is installed and running.

Dependencies using requisites

These states will run in the order they are defined in the file by default. However, we can also affect the ordering using **requisites**. Requisites allow us to create dependencies and interactions between our states.

The require requisite

The most basic requisite is `require`, which allows you to specify that one state requires another state to be run successfully first. Make sure that you note both purposes — the `require` requisite both ensures correct ordering and ensures that the requiring states run only if the required state ran successfully.

In this case, we want to make sure that `apache` is installed before we try to run it. So, we will add a `require` requisite declaration under our `service.running` state, as shown here:

```
install_apache:
  pkg.installed:
    - name: apache2

make sure apache is running:
  service.running:
    - name: apache2
    - enable: True
    - require:
      - pkg: install_apache
```

Note that we must specify both the state module `pkg` and the state ID `install_apache` when we define a `require` requisite. With this requisite in place, let's reorder the two state declarations in our `apache.sls` file and also introduce a typo. Note that in the following example, I'm trying to install `apache`, not `apache2`:

```
make sure apache is running:
  service.running:
    - name: apache2
    - enable: True
    - require:
      - pkg: install_apache

install_apache:
  pkg.installed:
    - name: apache
```

Now, if we run the aforementioned state, we will see our `require` statement at work, as shown in the following output summary:

```
# sudo salt '*' state.sls apache
myminion:
----------
          ID: install_apache
    Function: pkg.installed
        Name: apache
      Result: False
     Comment: The following packages failed to install/update:
     apache.
     Started: 23:32:42.579362
    Duration: 10073.515 ms
     Changes:
----------
          ID: make sure apache is running
    Function: service.running
        Name: apache2
      Result: False
     Comment: One or more requisite failed
     Started:
    Duration:
     Changes:

Summary
------------
Succeeded: 0
Failed:    2
------------
Total states run:      2
```

Note that the states were evaluated in the correct order and that the `service.running` state didn't run, because the `require` requisite state failed. If we fix our typo (change apache to apache2) and run it again, we see that everything will go green again, and that, once again, our states are evaluated in the correct order:

```
# sudo salt '*' state.sls apache
myminion:
----------
          ID: install_apache
    Function: pkg.installed
        Name: apache2
      Result: True
     Comment: Package apache2 is already installed.
     Started: 23:37:07.648991
    Duration: 649.11 ms
     Changes:
----------
          ID: make sure apache is running
    Function: service.running
        Name: apache2
      Result: True
     Comment: Service apache2 is already enabled, and is in the
     desired state
     Started: 23:37:08.298416
    Duration: 91.69 ms
     Changes:

Summary
------------
Succeeded: 2
Failed:    0
------------
Total states run:     2
```

The watch requisite

Now that we have a running Apache server, let's give Apache something to serve.

 For this example, we will enable a simple server status page. However, `apache2` on Ubuntu actually has this page already enabled. Before following the examples, we recommend that you disable this page with the following commands:

```
# sudo salt '*' cmd.run 'a2dismod status'
# sudo salt '*' service.restart apache2
```

To keep our example simple, we'll just create a couple of Apache configuration files that give our server a status page. To do this, we'll explore another state module that is very commonly used in Salt: the `file` module. Specifically, we'll use `file.managed`, a very flexible function to manage files on our minions. Here's what you get when you use the `file.managed` function:

```
# sudo salt '*' sys.state_doc file.managed
myminion:
    ----------
...

    file.managed:

            Manage a given file, this function allows for a file to
            be downloaded from the salt master and potentially run
            through a templating system.


        name

            The location of the file to manage


        source

            The source file to download to the minion, this
            source file can be hosted on either the salt master
            server, or on an HTTP or FTP server.  Both HTTPS and
            HTTP are supported as well as downloading directly
            from Amazon S3 compatible URLs with both
            pre-configured and automatic IAM credentials. (see
            s3.get state documentation) File retrieval from
            Openstack Swift object storage is supported via
            swift://container/object_path URLs, see swift.get
            documentation.  For files hosted on the salt file
            server, if the file is located on the master in the
```

directory named spam, and is called eggs, the source
string is salt://spam/eggs. If source is left blank
or None (use ~ in YAML), the file will be created as
an empty file and the content will not be managed

...

user

The user to own the file, this defaults to the user
salt is running as on the minion

group

The group ownership set for the file, this defaults
to the group salt is running as on the minion On
Windows, this is ignored

mode

The permissions to set on this file, aka 644, 0775,
4664. Not supported on Windows

...

For these states, we will need source files that the master will transfer to the minions as part of the state execution. By default, the master will serve all files (state files and other files needed by the minions) out of the /srv/salt/ directory that we've been using.

Let's create two files. The first is /srv/salt/mod_status.conf, the code for which is as follows:

```
<Location /server-status>
    SetHandler server-status
    Order allow,deny
    Allow from all
</Location>
```

The second is /srv/salt/mod_status.load, the code for which is as follows:

```
LoadModule status_module /usr/lib/apache2/modules/mod_status.so
```

Now, we will add two new state declarations to our apache.sls file to serve these files to our minion:

```
make sure apache is running:
  service.running:
    - name: apache2
    - enable: True
```

```
    - require:
      - pkg: install_apache

install_apache:
  pkg.installed:
    - name: apache2

sync mod_status.conf:
  file.managed:
    - name: /etc/apache2/mods-enabled/mod_status.conf
    - source: salt://mod_status.conf
    - user: root
    - group: root
    - mode: 600

sync mod_status.load:
  file.managed:
    - name: /etc/apache2/mods-enabled/mod_status.load
    - source: salt://mod_status.load
    - user: root
    - group: root
    - mode: 600
```

Here, we've introduced the `salt://` protocol in our `source` arguments. Those paths refer to files that the minion will request from the master. Again, these files are stored by default in `/srv/salt/`.

Let's test our new states! The output summary is as follows:

```
# sudo salt '*' state.sls apache
myminion:
----------
          ID: install_apache
    Function: pkg.installed
        Name: apache2
      Result: True
     Comment: Package apache2 is already installed.
     Started: 01:04:42.653416
    Duration: 662.55 ms
     Changes:
----------
          ID: make sure apache is running
```

```
    Function: service.running
        Name: apache2
      Result: True
     Comment: Service apache2 is already enabled, and is in the
     desired state
     Started: 01:04:43.316306
    Duration: 82.727 ms
     Changes:
----------
          ID: sync mod_status.conf
    Function: file.managed
        Name: /etc/apache2/mods-enabled/mod_status.conf
      Result: True
     Comment: File /etc/apache2/mods-enabled/mod_status.conf updated
     Started: 01:04:43.399299
    Duration: 155.956 ms
     Changes:
              ----------
              diff:
                  New file
----------
          ID: sync mod_status.load
    Function: file.managed
        Name: /etc/apache2/mods-enabled/mod_status.load
      Result: True
     Comment: File /etc/apache2/mods-enabled/mod_status.load updated
     Started: 01:04:43.555400
    Duration: 4.498 ms
     Changes:
              ----------
              diff:
                  New file


Summary
------------
```

```
Succeeded: 4 (changed=2)
Failed:     0
- - - - - - - - - - - -
Total states run:      4
```

Awesome! Let's see whether we can access our new server-status page:

```
# curl -Ss localhost/server-status?auto
<!DOCTYPE HTML PUBLIC "-//IETF//DTD HTML 2.0//EN">
<html><head>
<title>404 Not Found</title>
</head><body>
<h1>Not Found</h1>
<p>The requested URL /server-status was not found on this server.</p>
<hr>
<address>Apache/2.4.7 (Ubuntu) Server at localhost Port 80</address>
</body></html>
```

 Since our minion and master are the same machine, I used `localhost` in the previous command — if you are using different machines, you will need to retrieve the IP address for your minion and replace `localhost` with that IP address.

Uh-oh. Rather than getting the server status from Apache, we received a **404** status code! We forgot that after installing new configuration files for Apache, we must restart Apache.

Luckily, there's another requisite that will serve our purposes nicely: the `watch` requisite.

The `watch` requisite behaves in a manner that is very similar to that of the `require` requisite, with which we are already familiar. In fact, its base behavior is exactly the same: the watching state only executes if the watched state executes successfully first. However, if there are changes in the watched state (that is, if the "changes" piece of the watched state is nonempty), the watching state can add additional behavior.

In the case of the `service.running` state, this additional behavior is to restart the service in question.

Let's add two `watch` requisites to our state:

```
install_apache:
  pkg.installed:
    - name: apache2

make sure apache is running:
  service.running:
    - name: apache2
    - enable: True
    - require:
      - pkg: install_apache
    - watch:
      - file: sync mod_status.conf
      - file: sync mod_status.load

sync mod_status.conf:
  file.managed:
    - name: /etc/apache2/mods-enabled/mod_status.conf
    - source: salt://mod_status.conf
    - user: root
    - group: root
    - mode: 600

sync mod_status.load:
  file.managed:
    - name: /etc/apache2/mods-enabled/mod_status.load
    - source: salt://mod_status.load
    - user: root
    - group: root
    - mode: 600
```

Now, in order for the additional behavior to be triggered, we need to also change one or both of the files that are being watched. Let's add a blank space to `mod_status.conf`:

```
<Location /server-status>
    SetHandler server-status
    Order allow,deny
    Allow from all

</Location>
```

Now we need to run our state to see whether we have configured
everything correctly:

```
# sudo salt '*' state.sls apache
myminion:
----------
          ID: install_apache
    Function: pkg.installed
        Name: apache2
      Result: True
     Comment: Package apache2 is already installed.
     Started: 01:17:46.175205
    Duration: 775.938 ms
     Changes:
----------
          ID: sync mod_status.conf
    Function: file.managed
        Name: /etc/apache2/mods-enabled/mod_status.conf
      Result: True
     Comment: File /etc/apache2/mods-enabled/mod_status.conf updated
     Started: 01:17:46.952611
    Duration: 172.196 ms
     Changes:
              ----------
              diff:
                  ---
                  +++
                  @@ -2,4 +2,5 @@
                      SetHandler server-status
                      Order allow,deny
                      Allow from all
                  +
                   </Location>
```

```
- - - - - - - - - -
          ID: sync mod_status.load
    Function: file.managed
        Name: /etc/apache2/mods-enabled/mod_status.load
      Result: True
     Comment: File /etc/apache2/mods-enabled/mod_status.load is in the
correct state
     Started: 01:17:47.125025
    Duration: 6.316 ms
     Changes:
- - - - - - - - - -
          ID: make sure apache is running
    Function: service.running
        Name: apache2
      Result: True
     Comment: Service restarted
     Started: 01:17:47.220450
    Duration: 2338.367 ms
     Changes:
                - - - - - - - - - -
                apache2:
                    True


Summary
- - - - - - - - - - - -
Succeeded: 4 (changed=2)
Failed:    0
- - - - - - - - - - - -
Total states run:     4
```

Note that as expected, the service is restarted. Let's try querying the server once again:

```
# curl -Ss localhost/server-status?auto
Total Accesses: 0
Total kBytes: 0
Uptime: 44
ReqPerSec: 0
```

```
BytesPerSec: 0
BusyWorkers: 1
IdleWorkers: 49
ConnsTotal: 0
ConnsAsyncWriting: 0
ConnsAsyncKeepAlive: 0
ConnsAsyncClosing: 0
Scoreboard:
W_____...................
............................................................
............
Success!
```

The extra behavior that is added when there are changes in the watched state is defined in a special mod_watch function in the watching state module. Only a few state modules contain this special function, including the service, docker, mount, cmd, supervisord, test, and tomcat state modules.

We're not going to explore a real mod_watch function as it's out of the scope of this book. Please see the service state (salt/states/service.py) for a fairly straightforward example of how this function works.

Other requisites

The watch and require requisites are the most important and most used requisites in Salt. Here is a summary of the other requisites available in Salt, with a brief description of their use; exploring examples of each is out of our scope, but it's important to recognize that each one is available:

- onfail: This requisite is used to run a state only if another state has failed. It's especially useful for self-healing infrastructures and for rolling back code deployments after failure.

- onchanges: This requisite is used to run a state only if another state created changes. It differs from the watch requisite in that when there are no changes, it does not execute at all.

- prereq: This requisite is one of the most complex requisites. Let's assume that a service needs to be shut down (service.dead) before changes are made to a file, but only if changes will be made to the file. This is a use case for which prereq is perfectly suited. Basically, prereq allows a state to run only if another state is going to have changes when it is run in the future. We "look into the future" using a test run of the state that will possibly make the changes. See the Salt documentation for more details and examples.

- use: This requisite allows a state to inherit the arguments of another state, overwriting as necessary.

More information on these requisites can be found in the Salt documentation at `http://docs.saltstack.com/en/latest/ref/states/requisites.html`.

The _in requisites

States can also inject dependencies into other states. Each requisite has a version where _in is added to the end of the requisite (watch_in and require_in, for example). Requisites of this form force other states to depend on the state that contains the requisite.

An example is in order. Here is an excerpt from our original state where the service.running state requires the pkg.installed state to run successfully first:

```
install_apache:
  pkg.installed:
    - name: apache2

make sure apache is running:
  service.running:
    - name: apache2
    - enable: True
    - require:
      - pkg: install_apache
```

The following example is functionally equivalent to the preceding example:

```
install_apache:
  pkg.installed:
    - name: apache2
    - require_in:
      - service: make sure apache is running

make sure apache is running:
  service.running:
    - name: apache2
    - enable: True
```

The pkg.installed state is telling the service.running state to require the pkg.installed state. The resulting state execution will be identical in both of the previously shown examples.

Summary

States are very powerful and one of the most important pieces of Salt. In this chapter, you have written and executed your first states and learned about the structure of a state declaration. We then expanded our state declarations to enforce multiple pieces of state and created dependencies using requisites.

We've only just begun exploring states! In the next chapter, we will further expand our states using Jinja2 templating and pillar data.

5
Expanding Our States with Jinja2 and Pillar

In the previous chapter, you learned about the state system and wrote your first state. In this chapter, we will do the following:

- Learn the basics of the Jinja2 templating language
- Use Jinja2 to make our states platform agnostic
- Learn how to define minion-specific secure data in the pillar system
- Use Jinja2 to use pillar data in our states

Adding a new minion

The initial examples in this chapter will be all about cross-platform states. To make the examples clearer, we will add a new minion running CentOS 6.5. See *Chapter 1, Diving In – Our First Salt Commands*, if you need a refresher on how to install salt-minion on a new server. Here's a quick two liner to install a minion using Salt-Bootstrap:

```
# curl -L https://bootstrap.saltstack.com -o install_salt.sh
# sudo sh install_salt.sh
```

 Note that the easiest way to ensure the minion can easily communicate with the master is to have them both as cloud VMs rather than local VMs, so that they have individual, public-facing IP addresses.

After installing the same version running on your master, you should configure your minion to connect to your master's IP with the name centminion. Your /etc/salt/ minion configuration on your new minion should look something like this:

```
master: 69.164.192.51
id: centminion
```

Then, restart your minion, as follows:

```
# sudo service salt-minion restart
Stopping salt-minion daemon:                          [  OK  ]
Starting salt-minion daemon:                          [  OK  ]
```

Now, we can return to our master and accept the new minion's key so that we can communicate with it:

```
# sudo salt-key
Accepted Keys:
myminion
Unaccepted Keys:
centminion
Rejected Keys:
# sudo salt-key -a centminion
The following keys are going to be accepted:
Unaccepted Keys:
centminion
Proceed? [n/Y] y
Key for minion centminion accepted.
```

We know that we're successful if we can ping the new minion, as follows:

```
# sudo salt '*' test.ping
centminion:
    True
myminion:
    True
```

We can double-check that our minion is running a RedHat distribution instead of a Debian distribution by checking the os_family grain, as follows:

```
# sudo salt '*' grains.item os_family
myminion:
    ----------
```

```
    os_family:
        Debian
centminion:
    ----------
    os_family:
        RedHat
```

Everything seems to be in order! We're ready to discuss Jinja2.

Jinja2

Jinja2 is a templating language for Python. Templating provides a mechanism by which you can create content for files using code blocks to generate content dynamically. Jinja2 is modeled after the Django template language, so if you've ever developed in Django, the syntax should feel familiar. Even if you haven't, the syntax bears a resemblance to Pythons syntax, so it's not very hard to pick up.

There are two main types of Jinja2 syntaxes used in Salt. The first is variable, which uses double curly braces (the spaces around foo are for readability and are not required), and which is shown in the following code:

```
{{ foo }}
{{ foo.bar }}
{{ foo['bar'] }}
{{ get_data() }}
```

For these examples, the contents of the referenced variable or the results of the function call are placed in the document at the location of the Jinja2 block.

Jinja2 also has access to basic control statements. Control statement blocks use a curly brace and percentage sign, which is depicted in the following code:

```
{% %}
```

Here is an example of a conditional block:

```
{% if myvar == 'foo' %}
somecontent
{% elif myvar == 'bar' %}
othercontent
{% else %}
morecontent
{% endif %}
```

Here is an example of a loop:

```
{% for user in ['larry', 'moe', 'curly'] %}
It's user {{ user }}!
Hello {{ user }}!
{% endfor %}
```

We can also set variables for use later in the template, as follows:

```
{% set myvar = 'foo' %}
```

With these syntax basics, we're ready to use Jinja2 in Salt!

apache2 or httpd?

You'll remember that our `/srv/salt/apache.sls` file now looks like this:

```
install_apache:
  pkg.installed:
    - name: apache2

make sure apache is running:
  service.running:
    - name: apache2
    - enable: True
    - require:
      - pkg: install_apache
    - watch:
      - file: sync mod_status.conf
      - file: sync mod_status.load

sync mod_status.conf:
  file.managed:
    - name: /etc/apache2/mods-enabled/mod_status.conf
    - source: salt://mod_status.conf
    - user: root
    - group: root
    - mode: 600

sync mod_status.load:
  file.managed:
    - name: /etc/apache2/mods-enabled/mod_status.load
    - source: salt://mod_status.load
    - user: root
    - group: root
    - mode: 600
```

Let's try running this state on our new minion, as shown in the following command-line output:

```
# sudo salt 'centminion' state.sls apache
centminion:
----------
          ID: install_apache
    Function: pkg.installed
        Name: apache2
      Result: False
     Comment: The following package(s) were not found, and no possible
matches were found in the package db: apache2
     Started: 00:41:22.406646
    Duration: 3193.455 ms
     Changes:
```

Uh-oh! This looks like a problem. We'll discuss how to fix this shortly. The following is the continuation of the preceding output:

```
----------
          ID: sync mod_status.conf
    Function: file.managed
        Name: /etc/apache2/mods-enabled/mod_status.conf
      Result: False
     Comment: Parent directory not present
     Started: 00:41:25.602341
    Duration: 162.175 ms
     Changes:
----------
          ID: sync mod_status.load
    Function: file.managed
        Name: /etc/apache2/mods-enabled/mod_status.load
      Result: False
     Comment: Parent directory not present
     Started: 00:41:25.764635
    Duration: 5.494 ms
     Changes:
----------
```

```
        ID: make sure apache is running
  Function: service.running
      Name: apache2
    Result: False
   Comment: One or more requisite failed
   Started:
  Duration:
   Changes:


Summary
-----------
Succeeded: 0
Failed:    4
-----------
Total states run:    4
```

Uh-oh! Something went wrong here. It looks like the apache2 package is not available on our CentOS minion. If you're not familiar with CentOS, apache is actually installed using the package httpd on RedHat distributions.

We could solve this problem by writing another state file that uses httpd instead of apache2. However, that would be a lot of duplication of code and would be hard to maintain, and we would have to run our Debian and RedHat states separately.

Instead, let's use the power of Jinja2 to make our state platform agnostic by dynamically choosing the correct content for our state files.

The first step is to change the package name and service name depending on the grains of the minion. Luckily, Salt provides us with a grains dictionary in our Jinja2 templating. Here are the changes we will be making to the first two states in our /srv/salt/apache.sls file:

```
install_apache:
  pkg.installed:
{% if grains['os_family'] == 'Debian' %}
    - name: apache2
{% elif grains['os_family'] == 'RedHat' %}
    - name: httpd
{% endif %}

make sure apache is running:
  service.running:
```

```
{% if grains['os_family'] == 'Debian' %}
    - name: apache2
{% elif grains['os_family'] == 'RedHat' %}
    - name: httpd
{% endif %}
    - enable: True
    - require:
      - pkg: install_apache
    - watch:
      - file: sync mod_status.conf
      - file: sync mod_status.load
```

Let's try out our changes, as follows:

```
# sudo salt 'centminion' state.sls apache
centminion:
----------
          ID: install_apache
    Function: pkg.installed
        Name: httpd
      Result: True
     Comment: The following packages were installed/updated: httpd.
     Started: 00:48:43.521608
    Duration: 15986.367 ms
     Changes:
...
            httpd:
                ----------
                new:
                    2.2.15-31.el6.centos
                old:
            mailcap:
                ----------
                new:
                    2.1.31-2.el6
                old:
```

Yes, this looks much better. We now have `httpd` installed and the output continues:

```
- - - - - - - - - -
          ID: sync mod_status.conf
    Function: file.managed
        Name: /etc/apache2/mods-enabled/mod_status.conf
      Result: False
     Comment: Parent directory not present
     Started: 00:48:59.509440
    Duration: 285.603 ms
     Changes:
- - - - - - - - - -
          ID: sync mod_status.load
    Function: file.managed
        Name: /etc/apache2/mods-enabled/mod_status.load
      Result: False
     Comment: Parent directory not present
     Started: 00:48:59.795159
    Duration: 4.147 ms
     Changes:
```

Well, we're closer, but we're obviously not quite there. We still have some failures in our output. We'll figure out how to fix these shortly. Meanwhile, the output continues:

```
- - - - - - - - - -
          ID: make sure apache is running
    Function: service.running
        Name: httpd
      Result: False
     Comment: One or more requisite failed
     Started:
    Duration:
     Changes:


Summary
- - - - - - - - - - -
Succeeded: 1 (changed=1)
Failed:    3
- - - - - - - - - - -
Total states run:     4
```

As mentioned previously, we're getting closer—now at least, we have `httpd` installed on our system. However, as you can see, our `file.managed` states aren't working—it turns out that these directories are also different on RedHat distributions compared with Debian.

This is another problem that we can fix using Jinja2. Here is our `/srv/salt/apache.sls` file with all the revisions required:

```
install_apache:
  pkg.installed:
{% if grains['os_family'] == 'Debian' %}
    - name: apache2
{% elif grains['os_family'] == 'RedHat' %}
    - name: httpd
{% endif %}

make sure apache is running:
  service.running:
{% if grains['os_family'] == 'Debian' %}
    - name: apache2
{% elif grains['os_family'] == 'RedHat' %}
    - name: httpd
{% endif %}
    - enable: True
    - require:
      - pkg: install_apache
    - watch:
      - file: sync mod_status.conf
{% if grains['os_family'] == 'Debian' %}
      - file: sync mod_status.load
{% endif %}

sync mod_status.conf:
  file.managed:
{% if grains['os_family'] == 'Debian' %}
    - name: /etc/apache2/mods-enabled/mod_status.conf
{% elif grains['os_family'] == 'RedHat' %}
    - name: /etc/httpd/conf.d/mod_status.conf
{% endif %}
    - source: salt://mod_status.conf
    - user: root
    - group: root
    - mode: 600
```

```
{% if grains['os_family'] == 'Debian' %}
sync mod_status.load:
  file.managed:
    - name: /etc/apache2/mods-enabled/mod_status.load
    - source: salt://mod_status.load
    - user: root
    - group: root
    - mode: 600
{% endif %}
```

Note that the mod_status.load file is not even required on RedHat distributions. So, we use an if statement to make sure that whole stanza only runs on Debian distributions. We will also use another if statement around the watch requisite for that file.

Let's see whether we're successful! If we have done everything correctly, the states should run successfully on both our Debian minion and our RedHat minion:

```
# sudo salt '*' state.sls apache

myminion:
----------
          ID: install_apache
    Function: pkg.installed
        Name: apache2
      Result: True
     Comment: Package apache2 is already installed.
     Started: 01:04:15.934015
    Duration: 789.671 ms
     Changes:
----------
          ID: sync mod_status.conf
    Function: file.managed
        Name: /etc/apache2/mods-enabled/mod_status.conf
      Result: True
     Comment: File /etc/apache2/mods-enabled/mod_status.conf is in
     the correct state
     Started: 01:04:16.724719
    Duration: 143.022 ms
     Changes:
...
```

```
----------
         ID: make sure apache is running
   Function: service.running
       Name: apache2
     Result: True
    Comment: Service apache2 is already enabled, and is in the
    desired state
    Started: 01:04:16.869997
   Duration: 142.521 ms
    Changes:


Summary
-----------
Succeeded: 4
Failed:    0
-----------
Total states run:      4
```

Looking good! Our states are still running just fine on our Ubuntu machine, so we know we haven't messed that up. Here's the continuation of the preceding output:

```
centminion:
----------
         ID: install_apache
   Function: pkg.installed
       Name: httpd
     Result: True
    Comment: Package httpd is already installed.
    Started: 01:01:17.921195
   Duration: 492.866 ms
    Changes:
----------
         ID: sync mod_status.conf
   Function: file.managed
       Name: /etc/httpd/conf.d/mod_status.conf
     Result: True
    Comment: File /etc/httpd/conf.d/mod_status.conf updated
    Started: 01:01:18.415350
```

```
        Duration: 378.452 ms
        Changes:
                ----------
                diff:
                    New file
```

Double success! Not only are our states still working on Ubuntu, but we now have no failures against CentOS either! And the output continues:

```
----------
          ID: make sure apache is running
    Function: service.running
        Name: httpd
      Result: True
     Comment: Service httpd has been enabled, and is running
     Started: 01:01:18.794266
    Duration: 293.037 ms
     Changes:
                ----------
                httpd:
                    True


Summary
------------
Succeeded: 3 (changed=2)
Failed:    0
------------
Total states run:     3
```

Our states will now run successfully on any Ubuntu or CentOS machine, automatically detecting the correct information to send to each.

Defining secure minion-specific data in pillar

So far, we've only been defining the state of our infrastructure using state files. However, there is no mechanism in the state files for per-minion access control. Any file or data that you put in /srv/salt is immediately available for approved minions.

Thus, we need a system to give minion-sensitive data. That system in Salt is called the **pillar** system.

Much like grains, which we have talked about before, the pillar system is just a key-value store in Salt. However, each minion gets its own set of pillar data, encrypted on a per-minion basis, which makes it suitable for sensitive data.

Our pillar files are stored in a separate directory from our state files. By default, this directory is /srv/pillar. Let's create this directory:

```
# sudo mkdir /srv/pillar
```

```
# cd /srv/pillar
```

Let's define some pillar data. Inside /srv/pillar, we're going to create a couple of files. The first file is going to be /srv/pillar/core.sls. Note that pillar files also have the .sls file extension. Here are the contents of our core.sls file:

```
foo: bar
users:
  - larry
  - moe
  - curly
some_more_data: data
```

Note that these files, much like our state files, are defined using YAML. However, the structure of these pillar files is much more freeform. We're just defining data in the form of a dictionary. The data itself is arbitrary and will look different for most infrastructures.

Let's define a second file. Let's assume that we need to get a private SSH key down to one or more of our minions. That will be the purpose of this file. I'm going to generate a key just for the purposes of this example. I'll place the contents of the private key in a new file /srv/pillar/ssh_key.sls, as follows:

```
my_ssh_key: |
    -----BEGIN RSA PRIVATE KEY-----
    MIIEowIBAAKCAQEAr0y/hGfdFQHfs0fln6rToGFEQc9KCFA9fcpTRIwtRzVti
    +5NVjWDFvdyJPJ6L8RicUJ8fSjILOD60YTgUwfEqIp26GbWJ7BBZ+DAPjvPLW
    cEVpxqeSWeRZxVYJn9Rp/LgG/tnQtgy5LGawhdKFjXIBR2dN/jAJPJd4GkVn1
    ZmlfFsmitrCdlvg0T+hWfVe7jafEBUKfrSPd2haoBnraAyn31gb2xE9QdNsOK
    wRgfs/hvcxU2JuP3SIflD8ty6HHSk/p9wxxsm2SWtE0cGkwxPHbDpRU/V40CE
    9wnz2O5xhMxv+MhJygbvmbAuzCSqAFa0yv8SbwIDAQABAoIBABkbyhbB9bWrl
    00QCaNuA8xDmCvmT3KrmzvRzi4y2h2EwE7BhExDz+n7OVs3a+7plxWX5NLcg4
    grqmGLsKuvlIVD6YdQ/d67UT1Tapjsfjv8BcAOGWYO0FOyJ7x1cgSqoLBd18/
    CYXlk4UneT+gQ7ShhFdTNA98tpQ0fhE0Tledtt/89Y2tBCT48TfGI5qtByo/a
    pd7DjUfgWaP5B9pfKs1+Be3c1UvjU9IktdyLvu62CV8WZ+1uKebgGcotz5T80
    mWdBWyqtmfz4JOHyLpijM9IhS7CTPOOIc1dqMkK+haSivj7tOf+x6W7c6SX6c
    zBfxcGECgYEA1igfy6DMMWP/ObrKJNpH/dFLSsseSWomhy2w24Zr4L+PqU4cB
    kPdbrAayOcrsaV9OeE+mOEAQhH0s9WAGuT/8Kpf5lINsx4tVXad1HA7ZkpPmn
    JPPRkdLlNe/sdTbb0OrWw3G+uX0/Krn453RBCraYuVloELNz8/LnKHECgYEA0
    Ts6cs5Vlb24ZT6OKmZSjqZPTkBpTcO3VDuRT5m3aRNO7o4XTydIu8tHUF2FmS
    3trjZWiWyDaFJaVYQZPgjX1B/UyLtwTsWnI/esPGUGPd+IEe4NFIRGlMGrLYO
    /MhHUxEtXOkGMlrjGofYrkuPdENN0mp0Sxd8WN8CgYAXBWct15J7uLkl9otmX
    ZO5FswIFeFC99U5uust79Hu4AnqGtkzaP4zuOCYOil7RkPo5eq5um4xrAZ3En
    MQOlfILK0TnvVW4OzEKNipce56FB8VzCvicIGviizLDJhOUqVyRRDDgpbmpM6
    NowLX8eZHY5jRTcwwSrSMQKBgDNVwTpqJTtdUv8sUqkO4GplXn6xhzebK2vT5
    KIifysPntuUFaO/dPMEhpDqiEsQ1e+h1aRWzvJSJvq6NRgSyrGUdFWhvMx7/5
    kBWMFm41OQCi6SScQH756Ln1rEDvsUHr8oUoBRvovirh1xbtxqhUPG13+32bt
    tkqzAoGBAM7pH5+2uQ2ol/t6ucaf7UevtueWRuczpXrMzOYO/X1aWgK15HebV
    8XqjtNswquBcOjxrpgpGvr0IlkWNxR3RnC09fjr5hNs0ErCkbYjuex+1VB2yd
    QJgpe3uET6uiPNWSSewF6Er2RyC5D5ek232W8uEgWf5ULmX0qc68
    -----END RSA PRIVATE KEY-----
my_ssh_key_name: mykey.pem
```

This also serves to illustrate a syntactical concept in YAML. If you want to define multiline strings, you can use a pipe (see the first line) and indentation. YAML knows that the multiline string ends when you stop indenting the content. Thus, my_ssh_key_name (last line) is a new key in YAML because it's not indented.

Now that we have our pillar data defined, we need to tell the master which minions will receive which data. We do this using a special file, `/srv/pillar/top.sls`, which we call a topfile, as follows:

```
base:
  '*':
    - core
  'os_family:debian':
    - match: grain
    - ssh_key
```

There are a lot of new concepts in this file, despite it only being six lines long. The first thing you might notice is that the topfile is also formatted using YAML. It also follows a specific pattern.

The first level of indentation defines environments. We're going to gloss over that for now since we're only using the default environment, named `base`, at the moment. You will learn more about environments in *Chapter 6, The Highstate and Environments*.

At the next level of indentation, we define a series of targeting strings. Much like when we're targeting the command line (see *Chapter 2, Controlling Your Minions with Remote Execution*, to review targeting), the default is globbing, and we can override this default as needed. Thus, in this file, we're saying that all of our minions (`'*'`) will receive the pillar data in the subsequent list of files. In this case, there is only one file, `core.sls` (`- core`).

The second targeting string (`'os_family:debian'`) is a grain target. So, the first item in the list under that targeting string must define that we're using grain matching instead of globbing (`- match: grain`). Therefore, all of our Debian distribution minions will get the pillar data defined in `ssh_key.sls` (`- ssh_key`).

Pillar data is automatically refreshed whenever we run any states. However, it's sometimes useful to explicitly refresh the pillar data. We use a remote execution function named `saltutil.refresh_pillar` for this purpose. Here's how we explicitly refresh pillar data:

```
# sudo salt '*' saltutil.refresh_pillar
centminion:
    True
myminion:
    True
```

If we've done everything correctly, we can query our minions for their pillar data using the `pillar.items` remote execution function:

```
# sudo salt '*' pillar.items
myminion:
    ----------
    foo:
        bar
    my_ssh_key:
        -----BEGIN RSA PRIVATE KEY-----
        MIIEowIBAAKCAQEAr0y/hGfdFQHfs0fln6rToGFEQc9KCFA9fcpTRIwtRzVti
...
        8XqjtNswquBcOjxrpgpGvr0IlkWNxR3RnC09fjr5hNs0ErCkbYjuex+1VB2yd
        QJgpe3uET6uiPNWSSewF6Er2RyC5D5ek232W8uEgWf5ULmX0qc68
        -----END RSA PRIVATE KEY-----

    my_ssh_key_name:
        mykey.pem
    some_more_data:
        data
    users:
        - larry
        - moe
        - curly
centminion:
    ----------
    foo:
        bar
    some_more_data:
        data
    users:
        - larry
        - moe
        - curly
```

Depending on your version of Salt, you might also have another key in your pillar named `master`, which contains all of the master configuration options. This is dependent on a master configuration option named `pillar_opts`. Set this to `True` or `False` in your `master config` file (and restart your master) to determine whether the minions get this data as part of their pillar or not.

We see from this output that our minions have only the data we defined for them in our topfile. We can also query a specific pillar key using the function `pillar.item`, as follows:

```
# sudo salt '*' pillar.item users
myminion:
    ----------
    users:
        - larry
        - moe
        - curly
centminion:
    ----------
    users:
        - larry
        - moe
        - curly
```

Using pillar data in states

Let's finish up this chapter with an example that will show how we can use our pillar data in our state files using Jinja2.

Create a new state file, `/srv/salt/users_and_ssh.sls`, as shown in the following code:

```
{% for user in pillar['users'] %}
add_{{ user }}:
  user.present:
    - name: {{ user }}
{% endfor %}
```

```
{% if 'my_ssh_key' in pillar %}
manage_my_ssh_key:
  file.managed:
    - name: /root/.ssh/{{ pillar['my_ssh_key_name'] }}
    - mode: 600
    - contents_pillar: my_ssh_key
    - show_diff: False
{% endif %}
```

Note that we use a Jinja2 `for` loop to create a state for each user we need to add on our systems. We also only create the `ssh` key file if the minion has the correct pillar data using a Jinja2 `if` statement. Also note that we didn't actually use a source file for our `file.managed` call here; instead, we told the minion to just insert the contents of a pillar key in that file (`my_ssh_key`).

Let's run this state (I'm going to abbreviate the output in certain places due to space constraints):

```
# sudo salt '*' state.sls users_and_ssh
myminion:
----------
          ID: add_larry
    Function: user.present
        Name: larry
      Result: True
     Comment: User larry is present and up to date
     Started: 19:54:12.806207
    Duration: 0.982 ms
     Changes:
```

Remember that we added `larry` in a previous example, and so Salt doesn't do any work—it sees that `larry` is present and just reports success. Here's the continuation of the preceding output:

```
----------
          ID: add_moe
    Function: user.present
        Name: moe
      Result: True
     Comment: New user moe created
     Started: 19:54:12.807259
    Duration: 55.048 ms
```

```
Changes:
        ----------
        fullname:

        gid:
            1001
        groups:
            - moe
        home:
            /home/moe
        homephone:

        name:
            moe
        passwd:
            x
...
----------
          ID: add_curly
    Function: user.present
        Name: curly
      Result: True
     Comment: New user curly created
     Started: 19:54:12.862569
    Duration: 38.429 ms
     Changes:
        ----------
...
```

All of our new users were added successfully despite the fact that we only had to write one state declaration to accomplish it! That's the power of Jinja2 loops in your states. The following is a continuation of the preceding output:

```
----------
          ID: manage_my_ssh_key
    Function: file.managed
        Name: /root/.ssh/mykey.pem
```

```
        Result: True

        Comment: File /root/.ssh/mykey.pem updated

        Started: 19:54:12.901193

        Duration: 3.623 ms

        Changes:
                ----------
                diff:
                    New file


Summary
-----------
Succeeded: 4 (changed=3)
Failed:    0
-----------
Total states run:    4
centminion:
----------
          ID: add_larry
    Function: user.present
        Name: larry
      Result: True
...


----------
          ID: add_moe
    Function: user.present
        Name: moe
      Result: True
...
```

```
----------
          ID: add_curly
    Function: user.present
        Name: curly
      Result: True
...


Summary
------------
Succeeded: 3 (changed=3)
Failed:    0
------------
Total states run:     3
```

Note that our `ssh` key file was only created on our Ubuntu minion, as expected.

Summary

In this chapter, you learned how to make our states more flexible using Jinja2 templating. You learned the basic structures of Jinja2 and templated our apache state file so that it would run on both RedHat and Debian systems. You also learned how to define sensitive data in pillar and use that data in our states using Jinja2.

You now have all the tools you need to make flexible, modular states. In the next chapter, you'll learn how to better organize those files using topfiles in the state system, and you'll learn about environments in Salt.

6
The Highstate and Environments

In the preceding chapter, you learned how to use Jinja2 and pillar data to make your state file more flexible.

In this chapter, you will learn how to organize your states so that we can enforce the state of your infrastructure with just a single remote execution command.

You will learn the following:

- How to use topfiles in the state system to target state files to different minions
- How to use environments to further organize our state files
- How to use GitFS to store our state files in version control

The highstate

Until now, we have only been running a single state file at a time using `state.sls`. However, this doesn't scale very well once we have many state files to manage our entire infrastructure. We want to be able to split different pieces of our state into different files to make them more modular. How can we accomplish this?

In the previous chapter, you learned how to target your pillar files to different minions using a `top.sls` file or topfile. Topfiles can also be used in the state system to target different state files to different minions.

Let's create our topfile now, which is in /srv/salt/top.sls, as follows:

```
base:
  '*minion':
    - apache
  'os_family:debian':
    - match: grain
    - users_and_ssh
```

Note that this file is structured almost exactly like the topfile that we used for our pillar data. At the top level (first line), we define our environment. There will be more on environments later—for now, it's enough to note that the default environment is the base environment.

Within the environment, we define a series of targeting strings. Again, unless otherwise specified, the targeting string is using globbing to match minions. So our first match, '*minion', will match all of our minions because they all end with minion. The second targeting string has - match: grain beneath it, which means that it is using grain matching. It will match all minions that are running a Debian distribution of Linux.

Once we've saved the previous file, we're ready to run it. The complete set of state files included in the topfile is referred to as the **highstate**. Thus, it shouldn't surprise you that we use the remote execution function, state.highstate, to run the highstate, as shown in the following example:

```
# sudo salt '*' state.highstate
myminion:
----------
          ID: install_apache
    Function: pkg.installed
        Name: apache2
      Result: True
     Comment: Package apache2 is already installed.
     Started: 02:03:45.290738
    Duration: 1000.33 ms
     Changes:
----------
          ID: sync mod_status.conf
    Function: file.managed
```

```
        Name: /etc/apache2/mods-enabled/mod_status.conf
      Result: True
     Comment: File /etc/apache2/mods-enabled/mod_status.conf is in the
correct state
     Started: 02:03:46.292284
    Duration: 151.584 ms
     Changes:
----------
...
Summary
------------
Succeeded: 8
Failed:    0
------------
Total states run:       8
centminion:
----------
          ID: install_apache
    Function: pkg.installed
        Name: httpd
      Result: True
     Comment: Package httpd is already installed.
     Started: 02:03:45.673780
    Duration: 746.008 ms
     Changes:
----------
          ID: sync mod_status.conf
    Function: file.managed
        Name: /etc/httpd/conf.d/mod_status.conf
      Result: True
     Comment: File /etc/httpd/conf.d/mod_status.conf is in the correct
state
```

```
       Started: 02:03:46.420716
      Duration: 217.693 ms
       Changes:
----------
            ID: make sure apache is running
      Function: service.running
          Name: httpd
        Result: True
       Comment: Service httpd is already enabled, and is in the desired
state
       Started: 02:03:46.638601
      Duration: 81.936 ms
       Changes:

Summary
------------
Succeeded: 3
Failed:    0
------------
Total states run:     3
```

Note that everything was successful, and no changes were made, because we have
already run these states individually previously. Also note that on our CentOS
minion, which is a RedHat distribution, we only ran the states from apache.sls,
while our Ubuntu minion (a Debian distribution) ran all of the states because it was
targeted by both targeting strings.

> Note that if a minion is not targeted in the top.sls file at all, it
> will return an error when state.highstate is run.

Environments

Salt provides a concept of environments to further organize our states. Until now,
we've been using the default base environment. However, we can configure as many
environments as we need to organize our infrastructure and give each environment
its own location in the filesystem.

We configure the locations of our environments on the master in the master configuration file, `/etc/salt/master`. If you look for the `File Server Settings` section in the default master configuration file, you can see some example configurations. We're going to keep ours very simple and just add a single new environment. Somewhere in your master configuration file, add the following lines:

```
file_roots:
  base:
    - /srv/salt
  webserver:
    - /srv/web
```

In this case, we're using the example of configuring our environments for different purposes. We'll have our entire core configuration in our `base` environment and then we'll put the configuration for our web servers in the `webserver` environment.

Environments are designed to be very flexible and serve whatever purpose you want them to in your infrastructure. Here, we're using the example of different environments fulfilling different roles: maybe we would have an environment for our web servers, an environment for our database servers, and so on.

However, we could just as easily use environments in our rollout workflow, that is, we could have an environment for production, an environment for development, and an environment for staging.

Many users of Salt don't use the concept of environments at all and instead just organize everything within their `base` environment. This is also a perfectly valid use of environments, though it is recommended that you use directories to structure and separate the various pieces of your infrastructure to keep things organized.

To make our changes take effect, we need to restart the master, as follows:

```
# sudo service salt-master restart
salt-master stop/waiting
salt-master start/running, process 3340
```

Let's also create our `/srv/web` directory and move all of our Apache stuff into it, as follows:

```
# sudo mkdir /srv/web
# sudo mv /srv/salt/apache.sls /srv/web/
# sudo mv /srv/salt/mod_status.* /srv/web/
```

We don't actually need to modify `apache.sls` at all to make it work — since we moved the `mod_status` files into the new environment with `apache.sls`, it will be able to find those files just fine.

However, we do need to make some modifications to our topfile, `/srv/salt/top.sls`, as shown in the following lines of code:

```
base:
  'os_family:debian':
    - match: grain
    - users_and_ssh
webserver:
  '*minion':
    - apache
```

We can run our highstate to make sure that everything still works. The output should be pretty much identical — we haven't actually changed anything about the states that each minion executes; we've just changed where they're stored on the master. We will now run our highstate, as follows:

 # sudo salt '*' state.highstate

Note that we still only have one `top.sls` file even though we now have two environments. This is because even though the topfile lives in the same place as the rest of our states, it transcends environments because it defines environments.

You can have a different topfile in each environment; however, keep in mind that when you run a highstate, the topfiles from all environments will be combined into a single set of top data. So, it is recommended that you either have a single topfile in the base environment or have a topfile in each environment that defines only that environment.

An example would be useful. If I wanted to split the topfile from the previous paragraphs into its various environment pieces, we would have `/srv/salt/top.sls` looking like this:

```
base:
  'os_family:debian':
    - match: grain
    - users_and_ssh
```

We would also have our web server topfile in `/srv/web/top.sls`, and the following code would be its contents:

```
webserver:
  '*minion':
    - apache
```

Thus, when the two topfiles are combined once we run the highstate, there won't be any collisions as each topfile only deals with its own environment.

Environments in pillar

Environments work almost identically in the pillar system. We set up the environments in the master configuration, `/etc/salt/master`. We're not actually going to do much with the `pillar` environments in this book, but this is what our `pillar` environment configuration in the master configuration might look like:

```
pillar_roots:
  base:
    - /srv/pillar
  webserver:
    - /srv/pillar-webserver
```

The topfile also changes in the same way as the state system. It might look something like this:

```
base:
  '*':
    - core
  'os_family:debian':
    - match: grain
    - ssh_key
webserver:
  '*minion':
    - webserver_data
```

We could now make a `webserver_data.sls` pillar file in our `webserver` environment, and it would be applied to all of our `'*minion'` minions.

Expanding our base environment

Because we're treating our environments as roles, let's add some more "core" states to our base environment. One potential use case might be installing configuration files to our user on each of our minions so that if we ever log into those minions, we have all of our shell and editor configuration files. These files are often collectively named dotfiles, and I store mine on Github.

We'll start with our topfile, /srv/salt/top.sls, as follows:

```
base:
  '*':
    - myuser.user
    - myuser.dotfiles
  'os_family:debian':
    - match: grain
    - users_and_ssh
webserver:
  '*minion':
    - apache
```

Note that dots in state file names represent folders. This is to make them resemble Python imports. Thus, myuser.user actually points to myuser/user.sls.

My username on Github and the username I usually use on servers is basepi. That's the user I'm going to set up in my example.

Start by creating the directory, /srv/salt/myuser, as follows:

```
# sudo mkdir /srv/salt/myuser
```

Then, create /srv/salt/myuser/user.sls with these contents:

```
install_zsh:
  pkg.installed:
    - name: zsh

add_user_basepi:
  user.present:
    - name: basepi
    - shell: /bin/zsh
    - require:
      - pkg: install_zsh
```

These states will install **Z shell (Zsh)**, my shell of choice, add the user basepi, and then set that user's shell to Zsh.

Next, create `/srv/salt/myuser/dotfiles.sls`, as follows:

```
include:
  - myuser.user

install_git:
  pkg.installed:
    - name: git

clone_dotfiles:
  git.latest:
    - name: git://github.com/basepi/dotfiles.git
    - rev: master
    - target: /home/basepi/dotfiles
    - user: basepi
    - submodules: True
    - require:
      - pkg: install_git
      - user: add_user_basepi

install_dotfiles_if_changed:
  cmd.run:
    - name: 'python install.py -y'
    - cwd: '/home/basepi/dotfiles'
    - user: basepi
    - onchanges:
      - git: clone_dotfiles
```

These states make sure that Git is installed on our minions, clone my dotfiles repository from Github, and run my `dotfiles` install script whenever that `git` repository changes, (using the `onchanges` requisite). It also uses an `include` statement to ensure that the `basepi` user is installed first so that we can run the clone as the `basepi` user.

Let's run our new states! Our highstate output is getting quite lengthy, so I will cut out large swaths of the output to try to keep it to the new and relevant bits. Here's the output summary:

```
# sudo salt '*' state.highstate
myminion:
----------
...
```

```
----------
          ID: add_user_basepi
    Function: user.present
        Name: basepi
      Result: True
     Comment: New user basepi created
     Started: 21:33:48.700937
    Duration: 88.561 ms
     Changes:
              ----------
              shell:
                  /bin/zsh
```

...

Here, we see that our basepi user is added and that the user's shell is successfully set to the newly installed executable, /bin/zsh:

```
----------
          ID: clone_dotfiles
    Function: git.latest
        Name: git://github.com/basepi/dotfiles.git
      Result: True
     Comment: Repository git://github.com/basepi/dotfiles.git cloned to /
home/basepi/dotfiles
     Started: 21:33:48.793136
    Duration: 17718.574 ms
     Changes:
              ----------
              new:
                  git://github.com/basepi/dotfiles.git
              revision:
                  ade8cdf36f7414a2e4b82710e8c465b643627996
----------
          ID: install_dotfiles_if_changed
    Function: cmd.run
        Name: python install.py -y
```

```
   Result: True
  Comment: Command "python install.py -y" run
  Started: 21:34:06.512572
 Duration: 97.522 ms
  Changes:
           ----------
           pid:
               13081
           retcode:
               0
           stderr:

           stdout:
               Welcome to Colton's dotfile installation script!
               ('Please note that existing files will be renamed

               with a .old', 'extension, and existing .old files
               may be overwritten!')

               Please see disclaimer in source code before using
               this script.

               ('Installation of', '/home/basepi/.zshrc',
               'complete!')

               ('Installation of', '/home/basepi/.zsh',
               'complete!')

               ('Installation of', '/home/basepi/.vimrc',
               'complete!')

               ('Installation of', '/home/basepi/.vim',
                'complete!')
...
```

After our user is present, we're ready to clone my dotfiles repository with
git.latest and install the dotfiles in our home directory using the included
script. From the output, we see that the script was successful:

```
Summary
------------
Succeeded: 13 (changed=4)
Failed:    0
------------
```

```
Total states run:     13
centminion:
----------
...
Summary
-----------
Succeeded: 8 (changed=4)
Failed:    0
-----------
Total states run:      8
```

Success! We can see that all of our states ran without issue.

Storing our states in Git with GitFS

Up to this point, we've been storing all of our Salt files in folders on the master. Those files are then served by the master to the minions at their request. This fileserver system is actually a pluggable interface.

This means that we can store our Salt data in any platform we choose, assuming a Salt fileserver module has been written for that platform.

There are fileserver modules available for a variety of systems, including Git, Mercurial, Amazon S3, and SVN. The only one we'll be exploring in this text is the Git fileserver, or GitFS.

Showing a full example of how to set up a Git repository, add and commit states, and run those states is out of the scope of this book, so we will only be touching upon basic configuration details. If GitFS is of interest to you, feel free to try it out. Otherwise, you can skip this section. There is an extensive tutorial on the advanced features of GitFS in the documentation at http://docs.saltstack.com/en/latest/topics/tutorials/gitfs.html.

GitFS allows us to specify a remote Git repository from which Salt will fetch files. Branches in the repository will correspond to the Salt environments of the same name. The exception is the master branch; if it exists — the master branch becomes the base environment.

To configure GitFS, we must modify our master configuration file, /etc/salt/ master. There's a master configuration option called fileserver_backend. This is what fileserver_backend looks like by default:

```
fileserver_backend:
  - roots
```

The roots fileserver backend is the default backend representing files on the master filesystem. We could replace roots in this configuration with git if we wanted to exclusively use GitFS, as shown in the following code; or, we can use GitFS in addition to the roots backend by adding it to the list of fileserver backends:

```
fileserver_backend:
  - roots
  - git
```

If multiple fileserver backends are enabled, the master will search them in order when a minion queries for a file and returns the first match.

Once you've enabled GitFS, you must configure the remote repositories to which it connects. This is also in the master configuration:

```
gitfs_remotes:
  - git://github.com/saltstack/salt-states.git
  - file:///var/git/saltmaster
```

In the previous example, GitFS will query both a GitHub repository, github.com/ saltstack/salt-states.git, using the git:// protocol, and a repository located on the master filesystem, /var/git/saltmaster, using the file:// protocol.

In the example shown previously, with two repositories defined, the master will search the repositories in order to find the requested files, returning the first match it finds.

That's it! If you've set both fileserver_backend and gitfs_remotes correctly and restarted your master, your master will immediately begin serving files from the Git repositories you've defined.

This means that you can now store your state files in a Git repository, and Salt will automatically pull them from that Git repository as though the various branches were cloned into directories in /srv/, where we were storing our files earlier in this chapter. Salt continuously updates the Git repository with the latest commits, so you know that you're always running your latest state files.

Summary

In this chapter, you learned how to use environments and topfiles to organize your states. Now with a single command, you can enforce the state of your entire infrastructure with a single command.

After three chapters about the state system, you're now prepared to write simple and flexible states to define your own infrastructure.

From here, we will be exploring other features of Salt that will help manage your infrastructure. In the next chapter, we will explore Salt Cloud, and you will learn how to use it to manage your cloud servers.

7
Using Salt Cloud to Manage Virtual Minions

In the previous chapter, we finished up our exploration of the state system in Salt by learning about environments and the highstate.

In this chapter, we're going to explore another topic included in Salt, named Salt Cloud. You will learn about the following topics:

- How to configure Salt Cloud to talk to one or more cloud providers
- How to use Salt Cloud to create and bootstrap new virtual machines
- How to manage fleets of virtual machines using map files

Let's get started!

Setting up Salt Cloud

Salt Cloud is a project that was started to work closely with Salt to manage cloud virtual machines. As infrastructures move more and more to the cloud, it's useful to have an easy-to-use, powerful abstraction around cloud provider APIs that allows us to manage them with Salt.

Starting with the 2014.1.0 release of Salt, Salt Cloud is built into Salt, rather than being kept as a separate project. However, on certain distributions, you still might have to install the `salt-cloud` package in order to get all of the relevant files.

However, on our Ubuntu system, this is not the case—Salt Cloud was installed when we installed the Salt master. Having said this, depending on which cloud provider you'll be using, you might have to install `libcloud` using the following command:

```
# sudo apt-get install python-libcloud
```

Before we configure Salt Cloud, however, we need to decide which cloud provider we are going to use, set up an account, and get some information from that cloud provider.

In the examples in this book, we will be using Linode, a cloud host popular among developers. Depending on which version of Salt you are using, `libcloud` may or may not be a dependency for the Linode Salt Cloud provider. The version of Salt Cloud used in this book (2015.8.5) does not require `libcloud`.

 It should be noted that Linode is unaffiliated with this text and is not sponsoring its use in this book.

Setting up Linode

First, you must set up a Linode account to toy around with. Navigate to `http://linode.com` and click on the **Sign Up** button. The sign-up page is very simple, as you can see in the following screenshot:

Fill out the initial page, and Linode will send you an e-mail to complete the creation of your account. You will have to enter payment information and preload at least $5 into your account. Note that Linode bills hourly, so you should be able to experiment with Salt Cloud very cheaply as long as you delete the virtual machines afterwards.

Creating an API key

Once you're on your account landing page, you will need to create an API key for your account. In the upper-right corner of the page, click on **my profile**, highlighted in red in the following screenshot:

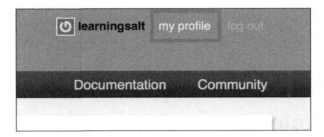

Enter your password when prompted and then click on **API Keys**, which is highlighted in red in the following screenshot:

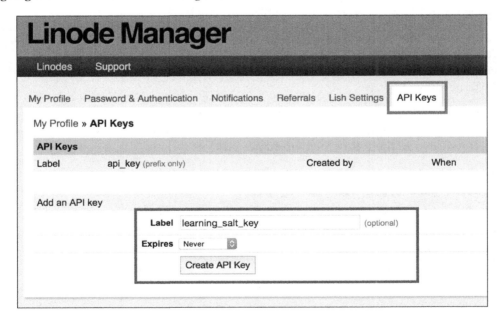

Then, fill in the required information to create an API key, which is highlighted in blue in the preceding screenshot, and click on **Create API Key**.

Record your key as instructed. The key I will use is highlighted in red in the following screenshot; you must use your own key as the key shown here will be disabled by the time you are reading this text:

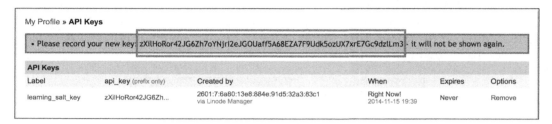

Now that we have our API key, we're ready to use Salt Cloud!

Creating a cloud provider configuration

Salt Cloud configuration files fall under two categories: cloud provider configuration and cloud profile configuration. The former is used to specify basic authentication information to access a cloud provider. The latter is used to specify specific virtual machine requirements, such as size, image, and location.

The cloud provider configurations go into /etc/salt/cloud.providers by default. Basic information about configuring each cloud provider can be found in the Salt Cloud documentation at http://docs.saltstack.com/en/latest/topics/cloud/config.html.

One of the pieces of information we need for the Linode configuration is an SSH key to access the VMs that we create. We can create an SSH key using the ssh-keygen utility, as shown in the following command:

```
# ssh-keygen
Generating public/private rsa key pair.
Enter file in which to save the key (/root/.ssh/id_rsa):
Enter passphrase (empty for no passphrase):
Enter same passphrase again:
Your identification has been saved in /root/.ssh/id_rsa.
Your public key has been saved in /root/.ssh/id_rsa.pub.
```

```
The key fingerprint is:
bd:7c:1c:36:65:42:95:f2:b9:9e:33:f2:e3:6c:63:fc root@localhost
The key's randomart image is:
+--[ RSA 2048]----+
|            ....  |
|             .. . |
|            .oo.  |
|        .   +o    |
|       S . +  .   |
|        . + o.    |
|         o oo .   |
|          ...@    |
|          *+*E    |
+-----------------+
# cat /root/.ssh/id_rsa.pub
ssh-rsa
AAAAB3NzaC1yc2EAAAADAQABAAABAQC/1vLlghC6RDC3WTDRk60X1v6rcgqPO1U/njc1c
gocUxYbB3qRg5VYE2hA190lR6vL9Xj5ASE4h/Xcgn0UVz316EUv91FNc1Tp11Ebvu9QF9
rR8CEQtPfbWXNdTzXNzJ3rJRgtL78/U3cju+aEH6y2JMX3nLFE7JcfNkSZ6zCGSI1tXfQ
tIrQd0B9vBFZBItcn5he1UL/LjEldyCR58z1t1Y0/LHqrxpYoOBC8Rz371B8Re32T9Hvs
5ZY1oMCVhZNYbBeFOxTcaW+fW8AufSdZPY93OFi8qNosKMF81ZF5D2CQG5qZ5Ri4hDaVM
Do+4HpOZkhtiqbHtDK0liiycGN1 root@localhost
```

Now, we have a key stored in /root/.ssh and know our public key, both of which we will need for our Linode configuration.

Here is what /etc/salt/cloud.providers will look like with our Linode configuration:

```
my-linode-config:
  provider: linode
  apikey: zXilHoRor42JG6Zh7oYNjrI2eJGOUaf...E7Gc9dzlLm3
  password: Learning Salt Is Fun!
  ssh_pubkey: ssh-rsa AAAAB3NzaC1ycA...tDK0liiycGN1 root@localhost
  ssh_key_file: /root/.ssh/id_rsa
```

Note that in the preceding example, I have shortened both my apikey and ssh_pubkey instances so that they will fit on the page. You should insert your full-length API key and SSH public key in those fields. Also note that you must specify a default root password to pass to Linode. You should make this password secure as root SSH login is on by default for Linode VMs.

We can verify that we haven't made any syntactical errors by doing some basic queries on Linode. These queries will also give us the information that we need in order to set up our first cloud profile.

First, using the `--list-sizes` option, let's list the virtual machine sizes that are available to us, as shown in the following example:

```
# sudo salt-cloud --list-sizes my-linode-config
[INFO    ] salt-cloud starting
my-linode-config:
    ----------
    linode:
        ----------
        Linode 1024:
            ----------
            bandwidth:
                2000
            disk:
                24576
            driver:
            extra:
                ----------
            get_uuid:
            id:
                1
            name:
                Linode 1024
            price:
                10.0
            ram:
                1024
            uuid:
                03e18728ce4629e2ac07c9cbb48afffb8cb499c4
...
```

Note that we also must pass in the name of our cloud provider configuration, `my-linode-config`.

Your output will be substantially longer—the only size that we're interested in is 1,024. As we can see, this particular VM size has 24 GB of disk space and 1 GB of RAM and, currently, it will cost $10 per month to run (billed hourly). This sounds perfect for our testing purposes.

Now we need an image to deploy on our VM. We can list the available images using the `--list-images` option, as follows:

```
# sudo salt-cloud --list-images my-linode-config
[INFO    ] salt-cloud starting
my-linode-config:
    ----------
    linode:
        ----------
        CentOS 6.5:
            ----------
            driver:
            extra:
                ----------
                64bit:
                    1
                pvops:
                    1
            get_uuid:
            id:
                127
            name:
                CentOS 6.5
            uuid:
                f12d308795a507cc73a3cf5f7aacdf2d86fbcf4a
        Ubuntu 14.04 LTS:
            ----------
            driver:
            extra:
                ----------
```

```
                    64bit:
                        1
                    pvops:
                        1
                get_uuid:
                id:
                    124
                name:
                    Ubuntu 14.04 LTS
                uuid:
                    18be6ebe9bb4f9a818f95a522ac213cfdf295e84
    . . .
```

Again, you will have many more images listed. Here, I have left two different images in the output that we will use. We can see that both of these are 64-bit images—one of Ubuntu 14.04 and the other of CentOS 6.5.

The last piece of information that we're going to need to create our cloud profiles is the Linode data center in which we will be creating the VMs. Here, we can use the `--list-locations` option, as follows:

```
# sudo salt-cloud --list-locations my-linode-config
[INFO    ] salt-cloud starting
my-linode-config:
    ----------
    linode:
        ----------
        Atlanta, GA, USA:
            ----------
            country:
                US
            driver:
            id:
                4
            name:
                Atlanta, GA, USA
    . . .
```

Atlanta sounds like a great location to spin up a few VMs.

Creating cloud VM profiles

We now have all the information we need. We are going to specify our VM profiles in /etc/salt/cloud.profiles, as follows:

```
ubuntu:
  provider: my-linode-config
  size: Linode 1024
  image: Ubuntu 14.04 LTS
  location: Atlanta, GA, USA
  minion:
    master: 69.164.192.51

centos:
  provider: my-linode-config
  size: Linode 1024
  image: CentOS 6.5
  location: Atlanta, GA, USA
  minion:
    master: 69.164.192.51
```

Most of this should be pretty self-explanatory. We specify which provider configuration we're using to spin up these minions and then the size, image, and location (the location is optional) of our VMs. The final piece is any minion configuration options we want to set on the new VMs. Here, we tell the new minions to connect to the master at 69.164.192.51, which is the IP address of my Salt master. Replace that IP address with the address of your master instead.

Creating and destroying machines

We can now use the profiles we've defined to spin up and destroy minions! Let's start small and create a single minion. We need to use the -p option to specify our cloud profile, and then give our minion a name as well. In this example, I will name my minion cloudminion01 and spin it up using the ubuntu profile I created previously, as shown in the following output:

```
# sudo salt-cloud -p ubuntu cloudminion01

[INFO    ] salt-cloud starting

[INFO    ] Creating Cloud VM cloudminion01

[INFO    ] Rendering deploy script: /usr/lib/python2.7/dist-packages/
salt/cloud/deploy/bootstrap-salt.sh

...
```

```
[INFO     ] Salt installed on cloudminion01
[INFO     ] Created Cloud VM 'cloudminion01'
cloudminion01:
    ----------
    _uuid:
        None
    driver:
...
    id:
        731884
    image:
        None
    name:
        cloudminion01
    private_ips:
    public_ips:
        - 50.116.43.66
    size:
        None
    state:
        3
```

Once again, I have abbreviated the output substantially. Salt Cloud will actually show all of the output of creating and bootstrapping the minion, which can be substantial.

 If you would rather redirect the output to a file, use the `--out-file` option with the `salt-cloud` command.

We now have a new minion named `cloudminion01` running Ubuntu. Even cooler, Salt Cloud actually preseeded the keys for this minion and accepted them on the master. From the moment Salt Cloud finishes creating the minion, it should be connected to our master!

Here's the code to perform what's outlined in this paragraph:

```
# sudo salt '*' test.ping
cloudminion01:
    True
myminion:
    True
centminion:
    True
```

Our new minion is there! We can now use all of our newly learned Salt tools to manage that server.

Let's create a few more minions, but this time, we will create multiple VMs at once in parallel mode using the -P flag, as follows:

```
# sudo salt-cloud -P -p centos cloudminion02 cloudminion03
[INFO    ] salt-cloud starting
cloudminion02:
    ----------
    Provisioning:
        VM being provisioned in parallel. PID: 18229
cloudminion03:
    ----------
    Provisioning:
        VM being provisioned in parallel. PID: 18230

[INFO    ] Creating Cloud VM cloudminion03
[INFO    ] Creating Cloud VM cloudminion02
...
[INFO    ] Salt installed on cloudminion02
[INFO    ] Created Cloud VM 'cloudminion02'
[INFO    ] Salt installed on cloudminion03
[INFO    ] Created Cloud VM 'cloudminion03'
```

Let's make sure that the new VMs are present, as follows:

```
# sudo salt '*' test.ping
cloudminion01:
    True
centminion:
    True
myminion:
    True
cloudminion02:
    True
cloudminion03:
    True
```

Success! We can also see these new minions' keys in the output of salt-key, which is as follows:

```
# sudo salt-key
Accepted Keys:
centminion
myminion
cloudminion01
cloudminion02
cloudminion03
Unaccepted Keys:
Rejected Keys:
```

In the next section, we're going to learn how to manage groups of VMs in a more stateful way using map files. So for now, let's delete the VMs that we've created. To delete VMs, you use the -d option for Salt Cloud. This is shown in the following example:

```
# sudo salt-cloud -d cloudminion01 cloudminion02 cloudminion03
[INFO    ] salt-cloud starting
The following virtual machines are set to be destroyed:
  my-linode-config:
    linode:
      cloudminion01
```

```
        cloudminion02

        cloudminion03


Proceed? [N/y] y

... proceeding

[INFO    ] Destroying in non-parallel mode.

[INFO    ] Clearing Salt Mine: cloudminion01, False

[INFO    ] Destroying VM: cloudminion01

[INFO    ] Destroyed VM: cloudminion01

[INFO    ] Clearing Salt Mine: cloudminion02, False

[INFO    ] Destroying VM: cloudminion02

[INFO    ] Destroyed VM: cloudminion02

[INFO    ] Clearing Salt Mine: cloudminion03, False

[INFO    ] Destroying VM: cloudminion03

[INFO    ] Destroyed VM: cloudminion03

my-linode-config:
        ----------
        linode:
            ----------
            cloudminion01:
                True
            cloudminion02:
                True
            cloudminion03:
                True
```

Just like this, our newly created minions are destroyed. Salt Cloud even took
care of deleting the keys from the master, as we can see from the following
output of salt-key:

```
# sudo salt-key
Accepted Keys:
centminion
myminion
Unaccepted Keys:
Rejected Keys:
```

Managing groups of VMs with map files

So far, our exploration of Salt Cloud has been limited to operations on single VMs or manually compiled lists of VMs. This is very useful but doesn't scale as well because there's no central source of truth for your VMs, especially if you have VMs across multiple cloud providers.

Salt Cloud provides a tool to solve this problem: map files. Basically, we create a map of our infrastructure and all the VMs that are in it. When a map is executed, your infrastructure will be brought to the state defined in the map file. Any VMs that already exist will be unmodified, and any new VMs will be created.

Let's create a map file to create multiple Ubuntu and CentOS minions. The location of the map file is unimportant, as we will pass in an absolute path to the map file anyway. Let's create it at `/etc/salt/mymap.sls`, as follows:

```
ubuntu:
  - db1
  - db2
  - web1
centos:
  - web2
  - load
```

As you can see, cloud maps are also formatted in YAML. At their most basic, they consist of just a list of minion names under the profile that will be used to create those minions.

For our map, we will be creating three Ubuntu servers, two of which are database servers (I haven't done anything special to differentiate the roles of these servers, except by naming them as Ubuntu servers), and one of which will be a web server. We also created two CentOS servers, one of which is going to be a web server, and the other is our load balancer.

Now that we have defined our map, we can execute on our map using the `-m` flag to the `salt-cloud` command. We can also pass in the `-P` flag here to have `salt-cloud` enforce the map in parallel. The use of these flags is shown in the following code:

```
# sudo salt-cloud -m /etc/salt/mymap.sls -P
[INFO    ] salt-cloud starting
```

```
[INFO    ] Applying map from '/etc/salt/mymap.sls'.
The following virtual machines are set to be created:
  web2
  load
  db2
  web1
  db1


Proceed? [N/y] y
... proceeding
[INFO    ] Calculating dependencies for web2
[INFO    ] Calculating dependencies for load
[INFO    ] Calculating dependencies for db2
[INFO    ] Calculating dependencies for web1
[INFO    ] Calculating dependencies for db1
[INFO    ] Since parallel deployment is in use, ssh console output is
disabled. All ssh output will be logged though
[INFO    ] Cloud pool size: 5
...
[INFO    ] Salt installed on web2
[INFO    ] Created Cloud VM 'web2'
[INFO    ] Salt installed on load
[INFO    ] Created Cloud VM 'load'
[INFO    ] Salt installed on db1
[INFO    ] Created Cloud VM 'db1'
[INFO    ] Salt installed on web1
[INFO    ] Created Cloud VM 'web1'
[INFO    ] Salt installed on db2
[INFO    ] Created Cloud VM 'db2'
...
```

We can now ping all of our new minions, as follows:

```
# sudo salt '*' test.ping
db1:
    True
web2:
    True
web1:
    True
load:
    True
db2:
    True
myminion:
    True
centminion:
    True
```

The cool thing about maps is that they're stateful. If we add a new minion to the map, it will only create that minion and leave the others alone.

Let's delete the VMs in our map using the -d option, as follows:

```
# sudo salt-cloud -d -m /etc/salt/mymap.sls
[INFO    ] salt-cloud starting
[INFO    ] Applying map from '/etc/salt/mymap.sls'.
The following virtual machines are set to be destroyed:
  my-linode-config:
    linode:
      web2
      load
      db2
      web1
      db1


Proceed? [N/y] y
... proceeding
```

```
...
my-linode-config:
    ----------
    linode:
        ----------
        db1:
            True
        db2:
            True
        load:
            True
        web1:
            True
        web2:
            True
```

Creating new masters with the map files

We'll wrap up our `salt-cloud` discussion by learning how to use the map files to create whole Salt clusters, including a master for the cluster, having all the minions connect to the new master.

Again, we create a map file. The location of this map file is irrelevant. Let's create it in `/etc/salt/mymastermap.sls`, as follows:

```
ubuntu:
  - mynewmaster:
      make_master: True
      minion:
        local_master: True
        log_level: debug
      grains:
        cluster: mynewcluster
  - newminion1:
      minion:
        local_master: True
        log_level: info
      grains:
        cluster: mynewcluster
```

```
        foo: bar
centos:
  - newminion2:
      minion:
        local_master: True
        log_level: warning
      grains:
        cluster: mynewcluster
        anothergrain: cool
```

There are a couple of new concepts in this map file. First, we have the `make_master` setting. This setting does exactly what you might expect—it makes that VM a Salt master. Then, for each of our minions (including the minion installed on our `mynewmaster` VM), we can use the `minion` setting to define minion configuration options. In the map files, `local_master` is a special setting to tell the minion to connect to whatever IP our new master VM is located at.

So, in this map file, we will create an Ubuntu machine that will have a master and a minion installed on it. The minion will connect to the master on that local machine. Then, we will create two more VMs, one Ubuntu and the other CentOS. Both of them will have the Salt minion installed on them and will connect to our `mynewmaster` Salt master as opposed to the master on which we're executing the `salt-cloud` commands. This means that we could easily create a whole Salt cluster, including master and minions, from a machine that will not be involved in the final cluster (for example, our laptop).

The final concept from this map is the `grains` setting for each VM. This allows us to set the static grain data on our new minions and can be any data that we choose.

I will leave the experimentation with this map file to you. Use the following command to execute the map file:

```
# sudo salt-cloud -m /etc/salt/mymastermap.sls
```

At the end of the run, you'll see data about each of your new VMs. Use the IP address of your new master to log in to the new master and play with the minions connected to it. Remember that you can delete all of those new VMs using the preceding command but with the `-d` flag instead of the `-m` flag.

Summary

In this chapter, you learned how to use Salt Cloud to make managing your cloud VMs and adding new Salt minions easy. You learned how to configure the Linode provider and create VMs that are automatically added to your Salt cluster, and how to use the map files to make your VM creation more stateful.

In the next chapter, you will learn how to use the event system in Salt to make a reactive infrastructure.

8

The Reactor and the Event System

In the previous chapter, you learned how to use `salt-cloud` to manage your cloud VMs.

In this chapter, you are going to learn how to make your infrastructure reactive and self-healing using events and the reactor in Salt.

You'll learn about the following things:

- The event system built into Salt
- How to fire events, both from Salt and from third-party applications
- How to create reactions to events

The Salt event system

Events are an integral part of almost everything Salt does. However, for the most part, these events are designed to be invisible and are designed to work behind the scenes to provide interprocess communication and make a complex system feel simple and friendly to the user.

We can also leverage the event system for our own purposes.

Listening for events

Before you learn about reacting to events or firing our own, let's inspect some of these events that are happening all the time in Salt. A Salt runner function (`state.event`) is provided for this purpose.

If we run it with no arguments, it will automatically connect to the master event bus and print all events that come through that bus:

```
# sudo salt-run state.event
```

Note that if you don't see any events, the easiest way to create events is by running a job (such as test.ping) from your master.

Here is the job I ran in one terminal window while state.event was running in another:

```
# sudo salt '*' test.ping
myminion:
    True

centminion:
    True
```

Here is an excerpt of the state.event output:

```
# sudo salt-run state.event
salt/job/20160513030202312339/new   {"tgt_type": "glob",
"jid": "20160513030202312339", "tgt": "*", "_stamp": "2016-05-
13T03:02:02.312623", "user": "root", "arg": [], "fun": "test.ping",
"minions": ["centminion", "myminion"]}

salt/auth   {"_stamp": "2016-05-13T03:07:55.004984", "act":
"accept", "id": "myminion", "pub": "-----BEGIN PUBLIC KEY-----\
nMIIBIjANBgkqhkiG9w0BAQEFAAOCAQ8AMIIBCgKCAQEAtHFZaLGBe71IIbjPyJGe\
n1fx/hTUJNMhT+O/Wh21YzdAN8JdQVgDLpevu+Ww5DoYQHrYnyoxI194foj35fEak\
nIoL2mA+aWBaAQrV6CI2I/PVMAL8uOOQfypuTQYyqHw9sj2zbGvDAS4zCrw8nUdtS\n1ZbPW
Ja5SwK5Xf3XsQDJFIfrGNAQLvdrv1DIYO8w6pTZgqVudb0cgU6gB2nL7g+y\nkwsXY4Ggzbi
NKVu1I0h8MRZM5bD73+XsesABgNoHuSXnpgRTWgVVrXoYjPhoNHxa\n66snGwK/w0rvEFuyTM
s6WG4+YsmKGRQkB0MdGLglrNpXkb51cAvxKuVVAQFYXQ2C\nUwIDAQAB\n-----END PUBLIC
KEY-----", "result": true}

salt/job/20160513030202312339/ret/myminion   {"fun_args": [], "jid":
"20160513030202312339", "return": true, "retcode": 0, "success": true,
"cmd": "_return", "_stamp": "2016-05-13T03:02:02.495713", "fun": "test.
ping", "id": "myminion"}

salt/job/20160513030202312339/ret/centminion   {"fun_args": [], "jid":
"20160513030202312339", "return": true, "retcode": 0, "success": true,
"cmd": "_return", "_stamp": "2016-05-13T03:02:02.500055", "fun": "test.
ping", "id": "centminion"}
```

If you look at the first event in the output, you can see that an event was fired when a new job was created. The event data contains the function that is being run (`test.ping`) as well as the arguments for that function, the minions on which the function will run, and so on.

Events formatted like the second event in the output are fired whenever a minion reauthenticates with the master. This can happen under a variety of circumstances, so you will see these types of events frequently on the event bus.

The final two events are the return data for our minions from our `test.ping` job. We can see the job ID (`jid`), the return data (`True`), and the fact that the job was successful. This event also contains information about the job that was run, which is similar to the initial event for a job, including the function and arguments for the job.

Event structure

Events are made up of two major parts. The event tag, which is used to identify the events, and event data.

As we see in our preceding event output, the tags look something like this:

```
salt/job/20141127001155262018/ret/myminion
```

Custom event tags should follow a similar pattern, using slashes to separate the identifiers—almost like a URL. From left to right, event tags usually get more specific. So, for the preceding event, we have `salt` as the first identifier, which is very general. From there, we have the `job` identifier, which tells us that this is job-related. Then, we have the job ID (`jid`) to tell us which specific job this event belongs to. Finally, we have `ret`, which tells us that this is return data, and the name of the minion returning, `myminion`.

Our custom tag might look something like this:

```
salt/custom/mycoolapp/failure
```

We might fire an event with this tag in the event of a failure within `mycoolapp` and could then have Salt respond by fixing the problem, notifying a system administrator, or performing any number of other tasks.

The second part of each event is the event data. Event data is arbitrary, JSON-serializable data formatted as a dictionary. We can put whatever data we want or need in the data field or even leave it blank if we don't need it.

Firing events from Salt

There are a number of ways to fire custom events in Salt. The first, and the easiest, is to use the event remote execution module. Specifically, we will use event.send, as follows:

```
# sudo salt '*' sys.doc event.send
event.send:

    Send an event to the Salt Master

...

    CLI Example:

        salt-call event.send myco/mytag foo=Foo bar=Bar
        salt-call event.send 'myco/mytag' '{foo: Foo, bar: Bar}'

...
```

So, let's use this in conjunction with the salt-call command to run the remote execution functions on our local minion in order to fire an event to the master event bus:

```
# sudo salt-call event.send 'salt/custom/mycoolapp/failure' '{"foo":
"bar"}'
local:
    True
```

In another terminal window, I had state.event running, and here's the event that was fired to the master:

```
salt/custom/mycoolapp/failure  {"data": {"__pub_fun": "event.send", "__
pub_jid": "20160513030755036183", "foo": "bar", "__pub_pid": 3072, "__
pub_tgt": "salt-call"}, "_stamp": "2016-05-13T03:07:55.046303", "cmd": "_
minion_event", "tag": "salt/custom/mycoolapp/failure", "id": "myminion"}
```

Perfect! Our custom event came through with the custom data we defined. Note that we can also see other information about the source of the event, including the source remote execution module function used, the job ID, and so on.

Firing events from custom code

Salt also provides an easy mechanism by which third-party applications and code can fire events onto the Salt event bus. Here is an example of how to fire events using Python:

```
# Import the proper library
import salt.utils.event
# Create and fire event
sock_dir = '/var/run/salt/master'
payload = {'sample-msg': 'this is a test',
           'example': 'this is the same test'}
event = salt.utils.event.SaltEvent('master', sock_dir)
event.fire_event(payload, 'salt/mycustomtag')
```

However, this example is a little bit limited in its usefulness as in order for the event to hit the `master` event bus, the example code must be run on the master.

It's much more useful to just use the Salt Python API in order to actually run the remote execution module, `event.send`, on the minion, as follows:

```
import salt.client
caller = salt.client.Caller()
caller.function('event.send',
                'salt/mycustomtag',
                {'foo': 'bar'})
```

When we run this script using Python, here is the event that we see (again, using `state.event` in another terminal window):

```
salt/mycustomtag  {"data": {"__pub_fun": "event.send", "__pub_jid":
"20160513031204207780", "foo": "bar", "__pub_pid": 3225, "__pub_tgt":
"salt-call"}, "_stamp": "2016-05-13T03:12:04.216211", "cmd": "_minion_
event", "tag": "salt/mycustomtag", "id": "myminion"}
```

More information on Salt's Python API can be found online at http://docs.saltstack.com/en/latest/ref/clients/.

Reacting to events

Now that you've learned how to fire our own custom events, it's time to learn how to react to those events. To accomplish this, we will use a tool, fittingly named the reactor.

The reactor is configured in two parts. The first piece is in the master configuration file and defines which events will trigger which reactor files. The second part consists of the reactor files themselves, which define the actions to be taken when reacting to events, and which are similar to the state files.

Here are the lines we will be adding to our master configuration file (/etc/salt/master):

```
reactor:
  - 'salt/custom/*':
    - salt://reactor.sls
```

Note that globbing is used to target multiple events with a single configuration. Thus, we are now set up so that when the master receives any event that has a tag that starts with salt/custom/, the master will execute the reactor.sls reactor file from our Salt files in /srv/salt.

> If multiple event matchers are defined, Salt will check them in order when an event is received, and it will run the reactor files associated with the first match.

Once you've saved the master configuration file, we will need to restart our master:

```
# sudo service salt-master restart
```

Now, let's create our reactor file at /srv/salt/reactor.sls:

```
remove_marker:
  local.cmd.run:
    - tgt: '*'
    - arg:
      - 'rm /tmp/marker'
```

The syntax here should look familiar as it follows the same basic rules as the state files. This is a very contrived example, but it will make it easy for us to see that it's working without inspecting logs. In this example, we tell Salt that whenever this reactor file is executed, it should run the cmd.run remote execution function, targeting *, with the 'rm -rf /tmp/marker' argument. We will be able to see that this file is deleted and thus know that our reactor has executed successfully.

Note the `local` prefix before `cmd.run`. This prefix is used to tell the reactor that it will run a remote execution command through Salt's local client. Alternatively, you can use the `runner` prefix to tell Salt to execute a runner, such as `state.orchestrate`.

Now that we have our reactor configured, we can trigger events and see the reactor at work. To test our general event reactor, we will create the marker file that it is configured to delete, then fire a `custom` event, and then see whether the file is removed:

```
# sudo salt '*' file.touch /tmp/marker
myminion:
    True
centminion:
    True
# sudo salt '*' file.file_exists /tmp/marker
myminion:
    True
centminion:
    True
# sudo salt-call event.send 'salt/custom/somecustomevent' '{}'
local:
    True
# sudo salt '*' file.file_exists /tmp/marker
myminion:
    False
centminion:
    False
```

As expected, the file was deleted when we received that event.

Next, we will extend the reactor file to have special behavior for a specific tag. Again, in `/srv/salt/reactor.sls`, we will write the following code:

```
append_tag:
  local.cmd.run:
    - tgt: '*'
    - arg:
      - 'rm -rf /tmp/marker'
```

```
{% if data['tag'] == 'salt/custom/mycustomapp/failure' %}
run_a_highstate:
  local.state.highstate:
    - tgt: '*'
    - kwarg:
        pillar:
          trigger_event_tag: {{ data['tag'] }}
{% endif %}
```

Note the use of Jinja2 in the preceding example. Just as with the state files, we can use Jinja2 to template our reactor files. We are provided with a `data` variable in Jinja2, which contains the data from the event that triggered this reactor file as well as the tag from the event, which we are using, as shown previously.

With this configuration, we tell Salt that when we receive an event with the specific tag, `salt/custom/mycustomapp/failure`, it should run a highstate on all of our minions. Perhaps we have set up our highstate to heal any failures in our custom app or perform similar functions. This means that when there is a failure, Salt will automatically fix the problem. We've also set up the highstate run to contain custom pillar information — specifically, the tag for the event that triggered the run.

In order to see that this highstate has occurred, we will have to inspect the job cache. For this purpose, I will use the `jobs` runner module. The last job in `jobs.list_jobs` should be our highstate run:

```
# sudo salt-call event.send 'salt/custom/mycustomapp/failure' '{}'
local:
    True
# sudo salt-run jobs.list_jobs
...
20141128051734805456:
    ----------
    Arguments:
        |_
          ----------
          __kwarg__:
              True
        pillar:
            ----------
```

```
        trigger_event_tag:
            salt/custom/mycustomapp/failure
Function:
    state.highstate
StartTime:
    2014, Nov 28 05:17:34.805456
Target:
    *
Target-type:
    glob
User:
    root
```

Using the job ID from the preceding output, we could easily query the job cache for the results of the highstate:

```
# sudo salt-run jobs.lookup_jid 20141128051734805456
```

We now have an infrastructure that can react to problems and changes without our interference! The uses and power of the reactor are nearly limitless—you could have it set up to do anything from paging an on-call admin to spinning up new servers and adding to your cluster. Salt provides the tools to react in just about any way that you can imagine.

Summary

In this chapter, you learned about the Salt event bus. You learned what events are, how to fire your own custom events, and how to set up Salt to react to specific events in specific ways.

In the next chapter, we will explore some best practices to secure your Salt-managed infrastructure and talk about specific security concerns when using Salt.

Security Best Practices in Salt

9

In the previous chapter, you learned how to use the event system and the reactor in Salt to make a reactive, dynamic, and auto-healing infrastructure.

In this chapter, you will learn best practices to secure your Salt infrastructure. You will learn the following topics:

- Security configuration options
- Key management
- Firewall and network configuration

Securing Salt configuration

The default Salt configuration values are designed to be pretty secure. However, sometimes, new users to Salt change configuration values for convenience, which could have an adverse effect on the security of your infrastructure.

Master configuration

open_mode and auto_accept

Salt provides the ability to bypass certain authentication protocols for very secure environments, or for convenience in testing environments. In your master configuration template, you'll find settings for open_mode and auto_accept:

```
# Enable "open mode", this mode still maintains encryption, but
# turns off authentication, this is only intended for highly
```

```
# secure environments or for the situation where your keys end up
# in a bad state. If you run in open mode you do so at your own
# risk!
#open_mode: False

# Enable auto_accept, this setting will automatically accept all
# incoming public keys from the minions. Note that this is
# insecure.
#auto_accept: False
```

At the first glance, these two settings seem very similar, and in many ways they are. The open_mode setting tells the master that it should skip the authentication step for any request. This means that any entity that tries to authenticate with the master will be accepted. Previously accepted keys under the same minion name will be deleted.

On the other hand, auto_accept tells the master to accept all prospective minions. However, subsequent requests are authenticated against the public key that was automatically accepted.

These settings do have their place. If your infrastructure is completely separated from the Internet, so that no malicious host could possibly contact your master, these settings can be quite convenient. However, I recommend you always keep these configuration options set to False for production infrastructures. Security is never convenient.

file_recv

The next setting we'll be discussing is also a master configuration option, file_recv:

```
# Allow minions to push files to the master. This is disabled by
# default, for security purposes.
#file_recv: False
```

This setting, if set to True, will allow minions to push files to the master. This can be very useful for transferring files from one minion to another minion with the master as the middle man. However, this also opens up a new vector for a malicious or compromised minion to push infected or malicious files up to the master.

Salt is designed to limit the impact that a malicious or compromised minion can have on the rest of the infrastructure. Compromised minions will have access to potentially sensitive data through pillar and will be able to request files from the master. But by default, the minion's ability to compromise the master itself, and by doing so compromise the rest of the minions, is very limited. Allowing minions to push files to the master gives compromised minions a way to attack and potentially compromise the master.

There are use cases for Salt where having the minions push files to the master is very valuable. Thus, there are times when setting `file_recv` to `True` may be worth the risk. However, for most infrastructures, this setting should remain `False`.

Peer publishing

Peer publishing is a very cool feature in Salt, which allows minions to publish commands to other minions. This can be useful when a minion needs to pull specific live data from another minion for its jobs.

However, this feature is disabled by default:

```
# Salt minions can send commands to other minions, but only if
# the minion is allowed to. By default "Peer Publication" is
# disabled, and when enabled it is enabled for specific minions
# and specific commands. This allows secure compartmentalization
# of commands based on individual minions.

# The configuration uses regular expressions to match minions and
# then a list of regular expressions to match functions. The
# following will allow the minion authenticated as
# foo.example.com to execute functions from the test and pkg
# modules.
#peer:
#  foo.example.com:
#    - test.*
#    - pkg.*

# This will allow all minions to execute all commands:
#peer:
#  .*:
#    - .*
#
# This is not recommended, since it would allow anyone who gets
# root on any single minion to instantly have root on all of the
# minions!
```

Enabling this feature is not inherently insecure. However, you should restrict peer publishing access to only the minions that need to execute the jobs and the specific execution module functions they need to execute. Remember that a compromised minion, which has been whitelisted for peer publishing, will be able to execute those commands on all other minions! The whitelisted commands can be used for destructive purposes, and an intruder could do a lot of damage.

In the previously mentioned comments, it is noted that you should not whitelist all commands for all minions. You should also not whitelist generic execution module functions, such as cmd.run. An intruder could use a function like this to run arbitrary commands on all your other minions, with root privileges!

Peer publishing is a useful feature, but should be configured with care. You should only allow minions to execute the exact execution module functions they need via peer publishing and should avoid execution module functions, which allow arbitrary command execution such as cmd.run.

Minion configuration

master_finger

In addition to the master configuration settings, there are ways to use the minion configuration to secure your infrastructure as well. The primary configuration value we will explore is master_finger, as follows:

```
# Fingerprint of the master public key to validate the
# identity of your Salt master before the initial key
# exchange. The master fingerprint can be found by running
# "salt-key -F master" on the Salt master.
#master_finger: ''
```

The discussion of this configuration value overlaps with our discussion of key management, which is to follow. If you set this configuration value to an RSA public key fingerprint, the minion will only connect to a master if its public key matches the fingerprint configured here. This is very useful for preventing your minion from trusting a malicious box that is masquerading as the master for your infrastructure. Once a minion trusts a master, it will give that master the equivalent of full root access to itself. Preconfiguring the trusted master key will make it harder for an attacker to execute a man-in-the-middle attack against your minion on the first connection.

Key management

Key management is another area of Salt with a vast range of convenience/security trade-offs. For convenience, Salt does not require you to manually transfer the keys between masters and minions in order for authentication to occur. Instead, the minion will contact the master, and the master will cache the minion's public RSA key, awaiting manual approval.

Often, if we just created the minion in question and a minion of that name appears in the master's key list, we can assume with some degree of certainty that the key we're accepting is the key of the minion we just created.

However, it's possible that a malicious party could have contacted the master under the same name. In this case, we would be accepting a key from a malicious party, who would now be able to retrieve data to which they should not have access.

Such an attack is unlikely. It would be very hard to execute, as it's a small attack window, and the attacker would need to know the name of the minion being created. However, in a secure production environment, it may be important to ensure the identity of this minion.

Preseeding the minion keys

Perhaps the most secure way of ensuring the identity of minions is to handle all key generation and exchange yourself, manually.

> There is a documentation page dedicated to this process, located at
> https://docs.saltstack.com/en/latest/topics/tutorials/preseed_key.html.

Rather than allowing the minion to generate its own key and present it to the master, we will just generate the keys on the master and deploy them to the minion before ever starting the minion.

To generate a key named myminion, we use the following command on the master:

```
# sudo salt-key --gen-keys=myminion
# ls
myminion.pem  myminion.pub
```

To preaccept this key on the master, we just must copy the public key to the accepted minions directory:

```
# sudo cp myminion.pub /etc/salt/pki/master/minions/
```

Then, you should transfer the private and public keys to the minion machine. We recommend using scp for this purpose. Once the keys are on the minion, we just need to put them in place in the minion's key directory:

```
# sudo cp myminion.pub /etc/salt/pki/minion/minion.pub
# sudo cp myminion.pem /etc/salt/pki/minion/minion.pem
# ls -l /etc/salt/pki/minion
total 8
-r--------  1 root root 1674 May  3 00:06 minion.pem
-rw-r--r--  1 root root  450 May  3 00:06 minion.pub
```

Note that the filename of the keys is important. On the master, the filename should match the ID of the minion. On the minion, the keys should be named `minion.pem` and `minion.pub`.

In the preceding command, you can also see that the permissions on the files are correct. The permissions on the public key are not very important, but it is very important that the permissions on the private key (`myminion.pem`) are restricted. That key has all the information a malicious party would need to authenticate with the master and retrieve all the secure pillar data for that minion. I recommend that the key be owned by `root` with `600` permissions.

Once the keys are in place on both the minion and the master, the minion will be able to authenticate with the master without any manual key acceptance, using `salt-key`.

Preseeding the master key

In the previous section, you learned about the minion configuration value, `master_finger`. This configuration value is the fingerprint for the RSA public key for the master and ensures that a minion only connects to the trusted master.

However, you can take this a step further by preseeding the master public key on the minion.

The master public key is located on the master at `/etc/salt/pki/master/master.pub`. You should transfer this key to the minion using `scp` or a similar utility and then copy it into a place in the minion's key directory:

```
# sudo cp master.pub /etc/salt/pki/minion/minion_master.pub
# ls -l /etc/salt/pki/minion
total 12
-rw-r--r-- 1 root root  450 May  3 00:27 minion_master.pub
-r-------- 1 root root 1674 May  3 00:26 minion.pem
-rw-r--r-- 1 root root  450 May  3 00:26 minion.pub
```

Note that the filename is important here as well. The master's key must be named `minion_master.pub`.

With this file in place, the minion will only connect to the master that has the matching private key to go along with the public key we just put in place. In fact, if a minion tries to connect to a master that doesn't match its cached public key, here's what will happen:

```
# sudo salt-minion
[ERROR   ] The master key has changed, the salt master could have been
subverted, verify salt master's public key

[CRITICAL] The Salt Master server's public key did not authenticate!
```

The master may need to be updated if it is a version of Salt lower than 2015.8.5, or

If you are confident that you are connecting to a valid Salt Master, then remove the master public key and restart the Salt Minion.

The master public key can be found at:

/etc/salt/pki/minion/minion_master.pub

[ERROR   ] Minion failed to start

Verifying with key fingerprints

Preseeding keys is the most thorough way to be sure that a minion and master are authentic. It's also a process that is fairly straightforward to automate.

However, as with most secure processes, it is inconvenient. Luckily, we can verify the minion/master identity using RSA key fingerprints instead. This will give us most of the security benefits while eliminating some of the inconvenience.

Master fingerprint

We previously discussed the master_finger minion configuration option. Salt provides a really easy way to retrieve the fingerprint:

```
root@vagrant-ubuntu-trusty-64:~# salt-key -F
Local Keys:
master.pem:   20:f3:30:07:e9:1d:d0:83:56:5b:35:fb:a6:d0:8a:2a
master.pub:   91:0a:e7:fb:37:40:5f:4a:6e:12:e0:c4:0a:8d:db:bb
Accepted Keys:
myminion:  d5:a8:47:03:ed:8d:94:e5:d7:34:22:2c:ad:96:1e:52
```

The Local Keys section is the one that interest us, specifically the public key. This fingerprint is the one we want to put in our minion configuration:

```
    master_finger: 91:0a:e7:fb:37:40:5f:4a:6e:12:e0:c4:0a:8d:db:bb
```

Now, the minion will only authenticate with a master whose public key matches this signature (and obviously whose private key matches this public key).

If the fingerprint doesn't match, the minion should fail to start in much the same way as it does when the cached public key doesn't match.

If you're following along with the 2015.8.5 version I used for the examples in this book, you'll see that there's a bug: the minion stacktraces, rather than failing gracefully:

```
# salt-minion
[ERROR   ] Exception in callback <functools.partial
object at 0x7fbb68467158>
Traceback (most recent call last):
  File "/usr/local/lib/python2.7/dist-packages/tornado/
ioloop.py", line 600, in _run_callback
    ret = callback()
  File "/usr/local/lib/python2.7/dist-packages/tornado/
stack_context.py", line 275, in null_wrapper
    return fn(*args, **kwargs)
  File "/usr/local/lib/python2.7/dist-packages/tornado/
ioloop.py", line 615, in <lambda>
    self.add_future(ret, lambda f: f.result())
  File "/usr/local/lib/python2.7/dist-packages/tornado/
concurrent.py", line 232, in result
    raise_exc_info(self._exc_info)
  File "/usr/local/lib/python2.7/dist-packages/tornado/
gen.py", line 1014, in run
    yielded = self.gen.throw(*exc_info)
  File "/usr/lib/python2.7/dist-packages/salt/crypt.py",
line 433, in _authenticate
    creds = yield self.sign_in()
  File "/usr/local/lib/python2.7/dist-packages/tornado/
gen.py", line 1008, in run
    value = future.result()
  File "/usr/local/lib/python2.7/dist-packages/tornado/
concurrent.py", line 232, in result
    raise_exc_info(self._exc_info)
  File "/usr/local/lib/python2.7/dist-packages/tornado/
gen.py", line 1017, in run
    yielded = self.gen.send(value)
  File "/usr/lib/python2.7/dist-packages/salt/crypt.py",
line 563, in sign_in
    self._finger_fail(self.opts['master_finger'], m_pub_
fn)
AttributeError: 'AsyncAuth' object has no attribute '_
finger_fail'
^C
```

Hopefully, in the current version of Salt, this bug will be fixed.

Minion fingerprints

You can also use fingerprints to verify minions before accepting their keys on the Salt master using `salt-key`. We hit on this briefly in *Chapter 1, Diving In – Our First Salt Commands*, when we accepted our minion's key, but we'll go over it here as well as a review.

You'll remember that when we first connect a minion to the master, its key is cached in the master's `Unaccepted Keys` section:

```
# salt-key
Accepted Keys:
Denied Keys:
Unaccepted Keys:
myminion
Rejected Keys:
```

To view that cached key's fingerprint, we can use `salt-key -f`:

```
# salt-key -f myminion
Unaccepted Keys:
myminion:  d5:a8:47:03:ed:8d:94:e5:d7:34:22:2c:ad:96:1e:52
```

Now we need to go to the minion in question and view its fingerprint:

```
# sudo salt-call --local key.finger
local:
    d5:a8:47:03:ed:8d:94:e5:d7:34:22:2c:ad:96:1e:52
```

Once we compare the keys and see that they match, we can accept the key for that minion without worry:

```
# salt-key -a myminion
The following keys are going to be accepted:
Unaccepted Keys:
myminion
Proceed? [n/Y] Y
Key for minion myminion accepted.
```

This process is less convenient, but it ensures that a rogue minion is never accepted into your infrastructure and given access to secrets and proprietary information. As always, it's a trade-off between convenience and security. Only you can judge the security needs of your infrastructure.

Firewall and network configuration

Finally, a short word on firewall and network configuration.

Salt is designed so that ports only need to be opened on the Salt master. This is convenient as the firewall settings only need to be modified on one machine. (Refer to *Chapter 1*, *Diving In – Our First Salt Commands*, for instructions on how to open the necessary ports on the master.)

However, this also means that we're opening ports on the most critical piece of our infrastructure. If our Salt master is compromised, the attacker could gain the equivalent of root access across our entire infrastructure!

Because of this single point of failure, it is recommended that your master should not be open to the public Internet, if possible. This is much less convenient, as external minions must be connected to the Salt master's private network (usually via a VPN), but makes it astronomically more difficult for an attacker to access the master.

If the master must be connected to the Internet at large, other failsafes can be put into place. For example, you might configure the firewall to only accept traffic from known minion IP addresses or subnets.

The takeaway here is that the Salt master is a powerful tool, but in the wrong hands, it becomes a terrible liability. Protect it!

Summary

In this chapter, you learned some best practices in order to secure your SaltStack infrastructure and some of the security concerns that accompany the convenience of a tool as powerful as Salt.

In the next chapter, you'll learn how to get involved with the open source Salt project.

10
How Can I Get Involved?

In the previous chapter, you learned some best practices to secure your SaltStack infrastructure.

In this chapter, you're going to learn more about the Salt open source project and how you can get involved.

You'll learn about the following things:

- How to create an account on GitHub
- How to find issues that need to be fixed in Salt
- How to clone the Salt repository and make changes to the code
- Some basic Git commands
- How to create a pull request
- How to get involved on the community mailing list and IRC

Contributing code using GitHub

GitHub is a website created to make open source software development easier. Most of the open source projects on the Internet are hosted on GitHub. This includes the code for the Salt open source project.

GitHub allows anyone to clone the repository for a project and make changes, and then propose that these changes be included in the main repository for the project.

Creating an account on GitHub

The first step is to create an account. Navigate to `https://github.com`, where you'll see the signup page:

Pick a username, e-mail, and password, and click on **Sign Up for GitHub**.

The project

Once you sign into your new account, you can check out the Salt project! It's located at `https://github.com/saltstack/salt`:

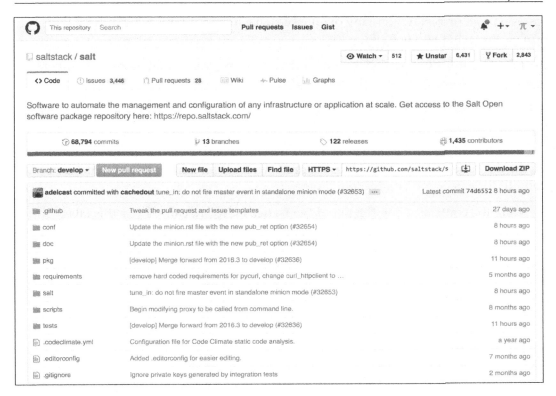

Here, you can browse the code for the project, view the outstanding feature requests and bugs in the **Issues** view, browse the project wiki, view Salt releases, and much more.

Since we're looking to contribute, a good starting place is the **Issues** view, which you can see in the following screenshot:

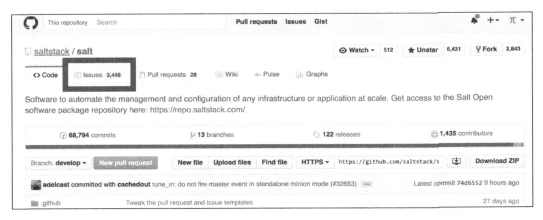

Salt is a large project, with many open issues. It can be a bit overwhelming if you don't know what you're looking for.

Luckily, GitHub supports labels, which the SaltStack project maintainers use liberally to allow for easier perusal of the issue list.

A list of the available labels and their meanings can be found in the SaltStack docs at `https://docs.saltstack.com/en/latest/topics/development/labels.html`. The label we're interested in right now is the **Help Wanted** label.

As the doc linked here states, **Help Wanted** is a label for simple issues that may be a good fit for a new contributor to the project.

By using the controls along the top of the **Issues** view, we can sort by this label:

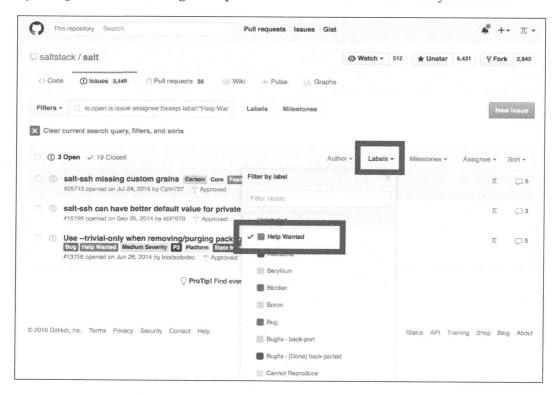

With the new shorter list of issues, we can look for an issue we're equipped to fix. Find a promising issue and click on it to see the details:

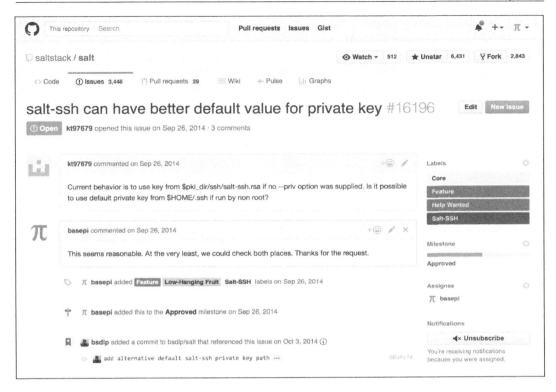

Getting the code

Now that we have an issue that we want to fix, we need to get the code. The first step is to **Fork** the Salt repository into our own repository in our GitHub account:

Now we have our own copy of the Salt code in our account, and we need to clone it to our machine.

GitHub is built on top of the version control software **Git**. Git is a subject big enough for many books, but my favorite primer on the software is the official book *Pro Git* by Scott Chacon, which is freely available on the Git website (`https://git-scm.com/book/en/v2`).

However, even if you don't have any experience with Git, you should be able to follow along with these steps:

1. First, grab the **HTTPS** clone URL from GitHub:

2. Then, navigate to a suitable directory in your terminal and clone the repository to your local machine. Make sure that you replace the URL in the `clone` command with the URL you copied from GitHub:

```
# cd src
# git clone https://github.com/basepi/salt.git
Cloning into 'salt'...
remote: Counting objects: 360894, done.
remote: Compressing objects: 100% (23/23), done.
remote: Total 360894 (delta 15), reused 4 (delta 4), pack-reused 360867
Receiving objects: 100% (360894/360894), 151.73 MiB | 773.00 KiB/s, done.
Resolving deltas: 100% (263751/263751), done.
Checking connectivity... done.
# cd salt
# ls
```

AUTHORS	MANIFEST.in	pkg	tests
COPYING	README.rst	requirements	tox.ini
Contributing.rst	conf	salt	
HACKING.rst	debian	scripts	
LICENSE	doc	setup.py	

3. We also want to make sure that we can always get the most up-to-date code from the official Salt repository, so we're going to tie our local copy to that upstream code by creating a new remote:

```
# git remote add upstream https://github.com/saltstack/salt
# git fetch upstream
remote: Counting objects: 10954, done.
remote: Compressing objects: 100% (8/8), done.
remote: Total 10954 (delta 4824), reused 4829 (delta 4824), pack-reused 6122
Receiving objects: 100% (10954/10954), 4.30 MiB | 937.00 KiB/s, done.
Resolving deltas: 100% (8212/8212), completed with 1335 local objects.
From https://github.com/saltstack/salt
 * [new branch]      0.11       -> upstream/0.11
 * [new branch]      0.12       -> upstream/0.12
 * [new branch]      0.13       -> upstream/0.13
 * [new branch]      0.14       -> upstream/0.14
 * [new branch]      0.15       -> upstream/0.15
 * [new branch]      0.16       -> upstream/0.16
 * [new branch]      0.17       -> upstream/0.17
 * [new branch]      2014.1     -> upstream/2014.1
 * [new branch]      2014.7     -> upstream/2014.7
 * [new branch]      2015.5     -> upstream/2015.5
 * [new branch]      2015.8     -> upstream/2015.8
 * [new branch]      2016.3     -> upstream/2016.3
 * [new branch]      develop    -> upstream/develop
 * [new tag]         v2014.1    -> v2014.1
 * [new tag]         v2014.1.0  -> v2014.1.0
...
```

Perfect. Our local development environment is ready. Now we just need to code the solution to our issue!

Contributing a fix

Salt has multiple development branches for concurrently maintained releases. This can make it difficult to figure out where a fix should be submitted. Luckily, the project maintainers provide guidance on this at `https://docs.saltstack.com/en/ latest/topics/development/contributing.html#which-salt-branch`.

If you're not sure whether your fix is a bug or a feature, you can usually use the labels on the issue as a guide. The example issue we're working on in this chapter is a feature request, so we want to submit our fix on the `develop` branch.

However, we don't want to code on our local `develop` branch. Instead, we want to create a new branch for each fix we make, so we can keep them separate and work on multiple fixes concurrently. Let's create a new branch for our fix, based on the upstream `develop` branch:

```
# git fetch upstream
# git branch issue_16196 upstream/develop
Branch issue_16196 set up to track remote branch develop from upstream.
# git checkout issue_16196
Previous HEAD position was b9d0336... Merge pull request #31964 from
jfindlay/2015.8
Switched to branch 'issue_16196'
Your branch is up-to-date with 'upstream/develop'.
```

Now we can make our changes.

Committing our changes

We can see that we have changes pending when we use the `git` status command:

```
# git status
On branch issue_16196
Your branch is up-to-date with 'upstream/develop'.
Changes not staged for commit:
  (use "git add <file>..." to update what will be committed)
  (use "git checkout -- <file>..." to discard changes in working
directory)
```

```
    modified:   salt/client/ssh/__init__.py
    modified:   salt/config/__init__.py
```

```
no changes added to commit (use "git add" and/or "git commit -a")
```

We can see the changes themselves with the `git diff` command (output truncated):

```
# git diff
diff --git a/salt/client/ssh/__init__.py b/salt/client/ssh/__init__.py
index f626858..d66e585 100644
--- a/salt/client/ssh/__init__.py
+++ b/salt/client/ssh/__init__.py
@@ -217,14 +217,18 @@ class SSH(object):
        # If we're in a wfunc, we need to get the ssh key location from the
        # top level opts, stored in __master_opts__
        if '__master_opts__' in self.opts:
-            priv = self.opts['__master_opts__'].get(
-                    'ssh_priv',
-                    os.path.join(
-                        self.opts['__master_opts__']['pki_dir'],
-                        'ssh',
-                        'salt-ssh.rsa'
+            if self.opts['__master_opts__'].get('ssh_use_home_key') and \
+                    os.path.isfile(os.path.expanduser('~/.ssh/id_rsa')):
+                priv = os.path.expanduser('~/.ssh/id_rsa')
+            else:
+                priv = self.opts['__master_opts__'].get(
+                        'ssh_priv',
+                        os.path.join(
+                            self.opts['__master_opts__']['pki_dir'],
+                            'ssh',
+                            'salt-ssh.rsa'
+                        )
                    )
-                    )
...
```

Now we need to make these changes official by committing them. We do this by using the git commit command:

```
# git commit -a
[issue_16196 9223f8e] Add a salt-ssh config to use homedir RSA keys
 2 files changed, 30 insertions(+), 14 deletions(-)
```

The preceding command tells Git to commit all changes to the files that Git is already tracking. When you run the command, Git will open your default editor and ask for a commit description. The first line of this description should be a short and sweet description of the changes, and a more verbose description can follow in the subsequent lines:

Once you save and exit your editor, Git will confirm that the changes were committed.

Pushing the changes and creating a pull request

Now that we have the committed changes on our local machine, we need to create a pull request in order to get our changes included in the upstream repository.

The pull request model may seem foreign at first, but it is integral to the process of developing open source software today. It allows anyone to propose changes to software, but allows the maintainers of the software to choose the fixes that actually make it into the code.

This is why we needed to create our own fork of the source code. In our fork, we can push whatever code we want and then request that our code be merged into the upstream repository.

We do this with the `git push` command:

```
# git push origin issue_16196
Username for 'https://github.com': basepi
Password for 'https://basepi@github.com':
Counting objects: 5579, done.
Delta compression using up to 8 threads.
Compressing objects: 100% (2173/2173), done.
Writing objects: 100% (5579/5579), 1.14 MiB | 1.13 MiB/s, done.
Total 5579 (delta 4440), reused 4465 (delta 3364)
To https://github.com/basepi/salt.git
 * [new branch]      issue_16196 -> issue_16196
```

 If you're using two-factor authentication, you'll need to generate a token to use as a password in order to push to GitHub over HTTPS. Alternatively, you can use the `ssh` keys.

Now our branch is available on our fork of the Salt repository on GitHub. We can view this branch using the **Branch** selection dropdown:

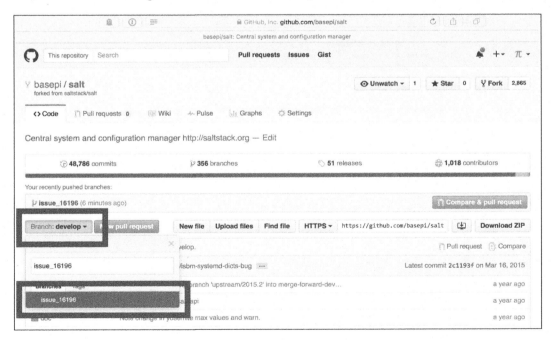

Once we are viewing the branch we just pushed, we can easily open a pull request against the upstream repository using the **New pull request** button:

The very first thing you should do once you see the pull request creation view is make sure that you're submitting the pull request against the correct branch. Earlier in this chapter, we determined that we wanted to submit our fix against the **develop** branch:

The Salt repository makes use of the pull request templates, so you'll note that there is a bunch of information already in the description box. Make sure that you give your pull request a descriptive title line and fill in the various sections of the description to give the maintainers as much information about your changes as possible. Then, click on **Create pull request**.

Now that your pull request has been created, the automated test will run. Watch the test area for the results:

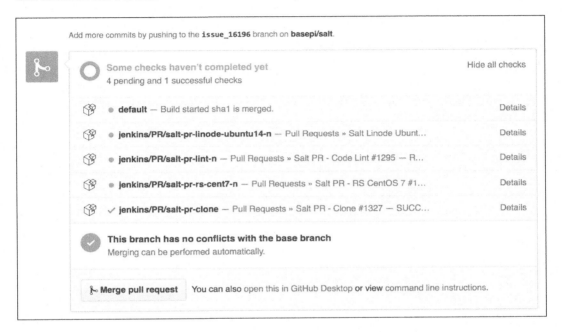

If there are failures, click on the details and see whether you can figure out where the failures are coming from. If you are unable to track the failures down, don't panic! The maintainers are very helpful and should be able to help you get things in order.

Make sure that you keep an eye on your pull request. In addition to test failures, the maintainers may have additional feedback you should follow. Once everything is in place, hopefully your fix will be merged, and you'll be an official contributor to Salt!

Other ways to get involved

Contributing code is not the only way to get involved in the Salt community. There are a few other ways that I want to talk about briefly:

- Salt-users mailing list
- `#salt` on freenode IRC
- `#saltstack` on the hangops Slack

Salt-users mailing list

The Salt-users mailing list is actually just a Google group. Head to `https://groups.google.com/forum/#!forum/salt-users`, where you can easily join the open group. Sign into your Google account (create one if necessary) and then click on **Join group to post**:

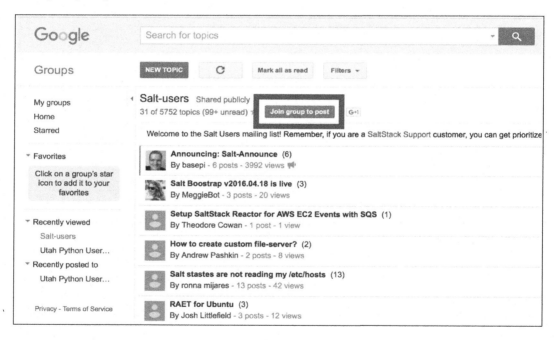

At this point, you'll have to make some decisions about how you want to receive e-mails from the group:

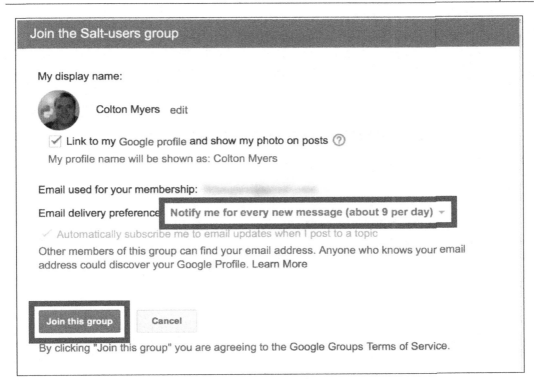

If you want to browse the group in the forum view online, you can choose to receive no e-mail updates. Alternatively, you can receive every update as it comes in or choose to receive summary updates to reduce the total number of e-mails you receive. Once you have your settings the way you like them, click on **Join this group**.

Now you send e-mail to the group by e-mailing `salt-users@googlegroups.com` or using the **New Topic** and **Reply** buttons on the web view. Remember that most of the users on the mailing list are volunteers, so you may have to be patient when waiting for solutions to the problems you post. As with any public forum, be courteous and respectful to the other members of the community. Jump in and ask or answer some questions!

#salt on freenode IRC

Much of the conversation around Salt happens on IRC. You can use your favorite IRC client to connect to `http://irc.freenode.net/` and join the #salt channel.

Alternatively, if you're not comfortable or familiar with IRC, you can just use the web client. Head to `http://webchat.freenode.net/?channels=salt` and choose a nickname for the **Nickname** field. Click on the **I'm not a robot** checkbox and **Connect**:

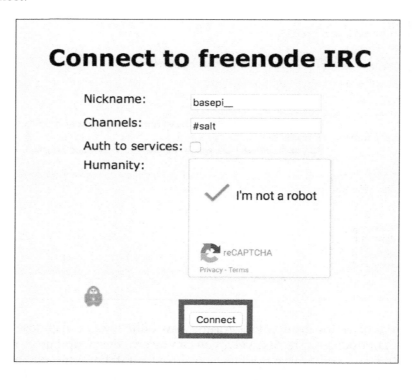

Be patient as it logs in and sets up your web client. Eventually, you'll see the `#salt` channel, where you can chat with other users and ask and answer questions:

As the topic for the channel notes, most of the people on that channel are volunteers and may not answer immediately. Stay connected and be patient!

#saltstack on the hangops Slack

Salt also has a channel on the popular hangops Slack. Slack is a messaging app for teams, and it works a lot like IRC, but with a more modern interface. You can sign up for an account with the hangops Slack team by navigating to `https://signup.hangops.com`:

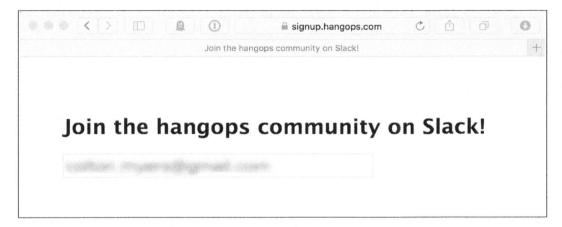

You will receive an e-mail invite to join the team. Follow the instructions, and eventually you'll be able to log on to the chat interface. Click on the **CHANNELS** heading and search for `#saltstack` to join the channel:

Now you can chat with other users of Salt in much the same way as IRC. Slack has unique advantages, such as the ability to read messages that were sent while you weren't connected.

However, there are fewer people on the `#saltstack` hangops channel than there are on the `#salt` IRC channel, so be patient when asking questions, and you will receive a response.

Summary

In this chapter, you learned about how to get involved with the Salt project. You learned how to contribute to source code, including finding issues to work on, committing code using Git, and opening pull requests. You also learned how to get involved socially by using the mailing list, IRC, and Slack.

This also brings us to the end of this book! You now have the skills to use Salt to begin solving problems in your own infrastructure. Remember that you can always find more documentation and information online at `http://docs.saltstack.com/en/latest/`.

The open source Salt project is sponsored and managed by SaltStack, Inc. Find more information about the enterprise support and products at `http://www.saltstack.com`.

Index

Symbols

_in requisites **84**
#salt, on freenode IRC **177, 178**
#saltstack, on the hangops Slack **179, 180**

A

apache2 **90-98**

C

code contribution
about 163
changes, committing 170-172
changes, pushing 172-175
code, obtaining 167-170
fix, contributing 170
GitHub account, creating 164
pull request, creating 172-175
Salt project 164-166
compound matching **32-34**
configuration management system, Salt **2**

E

environments, highstate
about 113-115
working, in pillar system 115
events
firing, from custom code 147
firing, from Salt 146
listening for 143-145
reacting to 148-151

execution modules

__opts__ function 52-54
__pillar__ function 52-54
__virtual__ function 50, 51
about 45-47
advanced example 57-61
cross-calling 48, 49
grains 50, 51
return data, reformatting 54-57

F

firewall **162**
Fully Qualified Domain Name (FQDN) **11**

G

Git
about 168
states, storing with GitFS 120, 121
GitFS
reference link 120
used, for storing states in Git 120, 121
GitHub
about 163
URL 164
using, for contributing code 163
glob matching **23-25**
grain and pillar matching **27**
grains
using 27-31
groups of VMs
managing, with map files 136-138